Table of co

CW00840689

Introduction

Woohoo! You've taken the first step towards financial freedom. Imagine what you can do with £1,000+ of extra wonga per year of disposable income, simply by not spending as much on your shopping bill. What would £1,000 in extra cash buy you? A holiday? Pay off some bills or debt? Mortgage deposit? Whatever it is, know this - it's achievable, and you don't have to be a crazed couponer with military precision to achieve it. Whatever goals you want to reach financially, it is there for the taking, so long as your mind is in the right place. Even if the savings add up little by little.

Now let's get something straight – this book won't contain frugal tips on saving the odd penny by using vinegar instead of cleaning products. The tips outlined in this book are ways to cut your spending on the essentials or things you already buy on a regular basis. By not spending as much on your essentials, you'll have more money left over to put to good use. £1,000s of pounds are vanishing from people's pockets year after year, so there is no better time to learn how to live paying under the retail price every time.

And that's why you're here. 100+ tips to cut over £1,000 off your supermarket spending each year. Because we're human – we need to go shopping... but we are a nation of bargain lovers. If you could get a bargain or freebie every time you went shopping, you'd be a very happy shopper. It's exactly that, which I'm aiming to teach you with this book.

Throughout this book, with every tip and method, I've included an achievable goal. These outline a simple way to put the tip you have just read into action. If every goal is achieved with each tip, you can reach a combined total of over £1,000 in yearly savings. This amount could be a lot more for bigger families. If you wanted a more chilled couponing experience, you don't have to follow each goal to the letter. Simply select whichever tips you want to use and save at your own pace. Little by little, these savings will add up to a huge amount of money, which can be spent on YOU, and not the supermarkets.

I started my money saving journey at just 15 years old. In my 6 years of cost cutting, I've saved over £10,000 across the board which otherwise would have gone into companies pockets. By seeking discounts wherever I go, that money has been put to good use in our family.

The money I've saved over the years has given me and my mother amazing life experiences we never thought possible. Thanks to couponing, the savings we have made has paid for:

- A new car without needing a loan
- A brand new boiler without needing a loan
- A week in Orlando staying at the Walt Disney World Resort for my 16th birthday
- A 5 night trip to Rome
- A 4 night trip to Barcelona
- A weekend in Disneyland Paris

Of course, it goes without saying... I got a discount on all of those purchases too (I try not to pay full price for anything!).

This just shows you what can be achieved when you put your mind to it. Now all you need are the tips to help you get there (and hopefully that's where I come in).

So strap in, hold onto your hats and get ready for a rollercoaster ride of money saving (just don't close your eyes, or you won't be able to read!).

Welcome to the world of extreme couponing…

But Jordooonnn...

"But Jordooonnn... I'm terrible with money. I just can't be helped, there's no way I can save as much as you".

Downright balderdash my friend – yes you can! There is no one and no thing on this earth that cannot be helped… (except for maybe a politician or two… I draw the line there!). You can save money if you put your mind to it. In some cases, just buying your same shopping through a different site or adding one more item to your basket could save you £100s a year. How easy is that? The first thing to start your money saving journey is your mindset. Positivity is the first important step towards financial freedom. The only thing you need after that is the knowledge of how to do it.

"But Jordooonnn... Doesn't couponing take ages? I just don't have the time to do it all".

Absolute codswallop 'ol pal! It can take up a lot of your time if you *want* it to, and you'd save more if you do, but there are plenty of ways to make huge yearly savings for not much effort. Even if you took one tip from this book, and used it to save £1 every week - that's £52 a year. May not be much to some, but for me… that's a lot of chocolate!

"But Jordooonnn… Do coupons really save you money? Aren't they just a marketing ploy?".

Not if you use them correctly. By releasing coupons, it is a way for manufacturers to get more customers. If you buy that product in the first place however, then you are saving money by using them. If you start buying dog food when you don't have a dog, just because you have a coupon for it - then that is unnecessary spending (it sounds crazy, but it happens. It gets that addictive!). Clever couponing and a bit of restraint will mean that you make savings, and not spend on things you don't need.

"But Jordooonnn… Isn't couponing only a thing in the US? You can't do it properly here can you?".

On the contrary! The UK has a bigger coupon market than you might think. Even though we only redeem around 1% of the amount the US does, you can still save some dough!

I'd argue in some ways, it's easier to maximise your coupons here than the US. For example, they don't have as many in-store sales as we do, and when they do, it's only on selected items. Pop into any supermarket on British soil and you'll find sale stickers down every aisle, with new offers starting multiple times a week.

So while the amount of coupons distributed might be less, if you do get them, you are more likely to match your coupons to an in-store offer to maximise your savings. US couponers have to strategise and comb through store inserts for what is on sale each week.

Yes, in the UK, supermarkets won't double your coupons, or pay you to take your shopping away like you see on the TV show 'Extreme Couponing', but there are still plenty of savings to be made.

My story

You might be thinking "who is this goofy looking kid, and how does he know so much about coupons!?" I hope you aren't, but let me tell you about myself.

I first started saving money as an awkward 15 year old boy. Even now at 21 years old, I still live by the things I taught myself at a young age. If a 15 year old can do this, then anyone can.

It was sparked mostly out of necessity, when my parents split up and my mother and I were worried about how we would survive financially. We loved going on family holidays and eating at restaurants, but on a single salary, it just didn't seem likely anymore.

Then, low and behold, we found a show on TV called 'Extreme Couponing'. It's a program about frugal shoppers in the US, who walk away with thousands of dollars of groceries for free, just by using coupons. From the first episode, I was hooked and decided to try it myself.

My mum, ever cynical, just thought this was one of my phases in life where I'd like it one minute and get bored the next. This wasn't the case. The second that the episode finished, I did a quick Google search, and printed out a stack to take into the supermarket that weekend.

This was probably the most excited a 15 year old boy had ever been going to the supermarket. I felt almost giddy that I'd walk out after paying with flimsy pieces of paper instead of cash. I entered the store with a beaming smile, around 10 coupons in my hand, and a mission to complete. I must have looked awfully strange.

With the products in my basket, it was time to go to checkout, and start scanning the coupons. When I started seeing the total drop, I knew that this was my calling. Every single beep was a thrill (and still is to this day!).

We managed to save a total of £5. The following week, I saved £10. The week after, £15. My savings through using coupons continued to grow.

Soon after, I started getting ambitious, trying even bigger shops. Some of my favourites include a £112 shop for just £32, our Christmas dinner for just 10p, and a £50 shop for completely free. All of which was achieved by a 15 year old boy.

Before this point, I never worried about money and wasn't taught much about it in school. This was certainly a huge wake-up call for me, but one worth waking up for (especially for a teenager who hated waking up).

Now a 21 year old teaching people how to save money as a full-time job, I practice what I preach and save money wherever I go. Thanks to learning these skills so early, I'm busy saving up to buy my first home (which could become a reality within the next couple of years).

This isn't a one-off either. Everyone can take back control of their finances and put £1,000s back into their pocket, by slightly changing your outlook and the way you spend your money.

Money saving inspiration

If you still aren't sold on the couponing lifestyle, here's the story of my biggest ever coupon shopping trip which got me over £1,000 of shopping for next to nothing!

It was the cold winter of 2013. Money was tight for everyone, especially with Christmas coming around. I remember seeing an article in a newspaper one morning reporting a record number of people would go without food on Christmas Day. For me, this was heartbreaking. What should be a festive and joyous time of year, would be miserable for so many that couldn't afford a decent Christmas.

I knew I had to do something to try and help, even if it was small. But what could a boy of my age do to make a difference? I didn't have money to donate and didn't have the manpower to change it. What DID I have? A knowledge of coupons and a folder packed full of them - that's what!

Took me some time to put two and two together, but I knew I wanted to use my couponing super powers to good use. Then it hit me. Spend the next few weeks collecting as many coupons as possible, to buy food for those who couldn't. What better way to hone in my skills and bring joy to those who otherwise wouldn't have it.

My mission was clear. I wanted to be ambitious and feed as many people with these coupons as possible on Christmas Day. I managed to team up with a homeless shelter, who the donated food would go to. I was shocked when they told me how many people they looked after… 150 people from 40 families. Yikes! What had I gotten myself into?

I didn't know if this was achievable, but there was no turning back now. All 150 people had to be fed. I couldn't fall short of helping each and every family. It turned into a task bigger than I imagined, but began my biggest couponing escapade yet, which I called… Feeding Forty Families.

The next few weeks were hard work. Not only was I still attending school, I was couponing from the moment I woke up, until the moment I closed my eyes. I'm ashamed to say, that even during some of my lessons at school, I was busy sending emails to manufacturers to get coupons - especially during I.T. (Sorry Miss Thomas… but it was for a good cause!).

I lost track of the amount of emails that were sent, calls were placed and coupons were printed. My fingers were sore from typing, and my ear must have had a phone print from how many calls I made. The amount of companies that loved what I was doing, and offered to send free coupons or products was amazing. In total, around 50 companies that I contacted sent me something to use for my big couponing shop.

Over the next few weeks, my house was the postman's busiest address. Something turned up every day, from £40 worth of coupons to a 20kg bag of rice. Typically, the gigantic bag of rice turned up when nobody was home, and was left with my neighbour, which meant me dragging it back to my place. Imagine me, a skinny 16 year old boy, with practically no muscle, trying to carry that into my house. It wasn't a pretty sight!

Along with the donated items and coupons, I went through nearly a whole ream of paper printing coupons off. The higher the coupons stacked, the more likely it was that they might actually pay for 150 people to eat on Christmas Day.

When everything had arrived, I had over 450 coupons to redeem worth £592, and over £600 in donated food items sent directly from manufacturers. Slowly, everything was coming together.

The day of the shop came round, what a big day it was. My alarm buzzed at 5:00am on Monday 16th December. Yes, you did read correctly, a 16 year old up at 5:00am. Even my own body didn't believe it!

After hours of preparation, research, phone calls and a few paper cuts, I was finally in the supermarket and ready to spend my hard earned coupons. When I walked in with the same beaming smile as my first couponing trip, who knew that this trip would change my life.

You'd be lying if you've never dreamed of doing a mad trolley dash through a supermarket. This is something I got to experience in this shopping trip. Finding over 500 items and putting them all in the trolley would take some time. A trolley dash was highly necessary (honest!).

It took nearly two hours to round everything up. I wasn't alone either, I had an amazing group of helpers with their own lists too… and it still took two hours! That shows you the scale of how much food we had to buy (and pay nothing for!).

Picture in your mind, three huge shopping trolleys filled to the brim with food, all being pushed by me. With only two arms, it was difficult to steer them all. I tried the 'two arms and a leg' method to push all three at once, which didn't work too well. Neither did pushing one trolley, with the other two stacked ahead of it in one long row. To say I got funny looks was an understatement!

After carefully pushing my haul to the till… the time had come. But first came the painful process of loading all 500 items onto the conveyer, and I mean *literally* painful. I was up and down like a yo-yo from the trolley to conveyer. On several occasions I managed to miss, and drop several items on the floor too, which didn't help my back! My nickname is clumsy Cox... take that how you will!

As the beeps kept coming of items being scanned, the total rocked up. The final bill revealed our grand total… £572. Yikes! I'd never even seen that much money before. Good job I had mum there in case things went wrong.

Nothing can beat 'that look' you get when handing over 450+ coupons to the cashier to pay for your shopping. It's not a moment shared by many, but it's a memory engrained in my head ever since. Her face was a picture… I should have framed it!

As that five inch thick wad of coupons started to be scanned, every single beep meant I was saving money… and there were a lot of them! As you can imagine, it took a while to get through every one, and at this point, we'd already been shopping for over three hours.

After nearly another two hours of beeps, heavy breathing and a little sweating, the total was under £10. Even this was an amazing feat. I wasn't done yet though. Despite all of this, there were still £30 worth of coupons to be scanned and only £10 left of my total. Somehow in all the chaos, I'd misjudged my costing, and ended up being £20 under.

In the UK, supermarkets will never pay you back if your coupons go over the value of your shopping, so this meant another supermarket trolley dash through one of the biggest Tesco Superstores in London to find £20 more worth of products to add to the shop.

Being a perfectionist, I wanted my total to be zero. So there I was, frantically adding up prices in my head as I waddled around the shop with packs of potatoes, parsnips and 10p sweets in my arms. This was no time to get a basket, this was my final coupon-down!

Plonking all of the items in my arms down on the conveyer, I breathed a sigh of relief thinking it would all end up free. The cashier started to scan the new items in. I have never watched potatoes being scanned through with such passion on my face. If people in that shop didn't think I was crazy before, they did now.

Everything was scanned, pushing the total back up to £30, with roughly £30 worth of coupons left. It was time for the final coupons to do their magic.

£5… £4… £3… £2… The last coupon… **BEEP**. Still £2. It didn't scan. Out of all 450+ coupons, the one that went wrong HAD to be the last one didn't it?! They tried the coupon again… **BEEP**. The total dropped, and the coupon had worked. The coupon's value? £1.96.

After five hours of shopping, the total came to just 4p. Nearly £600 worth of groceries that cost mere pocket change. Was I pleased? Of course. Did that last 4p disappoint me? Yes, it absolutely killed me! The fact that I'd achieved what seemed an unreachable goal of feeding 150 people totally on coupons was incredible… but it would've been that little bit sweeter if it was totally free.

Despite the mad trolley dashes and frantic maths, that's easily the best 4p I've ever spent. A total of 40 families would now be having a cooked Christmas meal, all thanks to coupons. To this day, I look back on it with pride. Big thank you to the cashier on shift that day – I expect that wasn't a normal work day for her either!

The week that followed that fateful shop was even busier than the last, that's because the press found out. Suddenly the tables had turned, now MY phone was constantly ringing. Nearly every UK newspaper wrote an article about the shopping trip, and it even managed to circulate around the world, with people tweeting about it in Swedish, Chinese and Spanish. Let's hope they didn't say anything bad, because I couldn't understand a word!

From reading one article, and using my coupon knowledge to good use, one boy with a folder full of coupons, changed the lives of 150 people, and influenced 1,000s others to start taking hold of their money.

This just shows what one voice can do, no matter how small. The whole experience was a real game changer, and made me more dedicated to help others achieve the same things. Not everyone will do £600 worth of coupon shopping, but even the simplest tips to cut your food bill, will put more money back in your pocket. This is the reason you have this book in your hands today.

There is a lot to learn to reduce your bills, and this book will only cover a small portion of it all. I hope my crazy story has inspired you to get started on your cost cutting journey. Even if you learn just one thing from this book by having me as your money saving advisor, then I'd be extremely happy. So let's not waste any more time. This is the start of your journey to financial freedom, and putting your hard earned money back into your pocket. Happy saving!

How to save £1,000s on your supermarket shopping

Let's get down to the nitty gritty. You don't *ever* have to pay full price for your supermarket shopping, though so many people do. The reason why is lack of knowledge. Most normal shoppers don't know that by picking up a supermarket magazine just before you paid, you can rip out coupons to save money on your shop. They don't know that by downloading apps on your phone, you can halve the price of your shopping bill. And they never thought to contact brands and make £100s from simple emailing.

When it comes to couponing, there is not one set way of doing it. Everyone has their own styles and select the tips they want to take on. That's what makes this such a rewarding hobby for most. Yes, it might take a bit of time, but it's a hobby that pays YOU, instead of the other way around.

If you ever go to the supermarket and the total comes out way more than you expected and think "oh dear! I need to keep tabs next time." don't worry. You're in safe hands now.

There are plenty of ways to cut down costs in the supermarket, from coupons to price comparisons – and it doesn't take that much time. As long as you have the right mind-set, and want to pay less for the same items – with these tips, you will.

Coupons

One of my favourite words in the world as a money saver - 'coupons'! Just by using this paper money when you go shopping can save you a lot of cash… and I mean A LOT.

In a nutshell, a coupon is a piece of paper that you hand over at the supermarket till to get money off an item. Most of the time it is an amount off (like 50p off, £1 off) and it is scanned at checkout to get you a discount.

Coupons are scattered all over, and despite what you might think, they do save you money, and they are for things you'd normally use… if you know how to coupon efficiently.

There's a lot to cover in the couponing world, including some major do's and don'ts to aid you on your cost cutting journey. So strap in, and get ready for the money saving ride of your life!

History of coupons

Couponing started in the US in 1888 for a new drink called "Coca Cola" encouraging people to buy it. Hard to believe right? But it worked a treat. They sent out millions of coupons to people's homes and put them in newspapers. It was estimated that 1 in 9 Americans claimed a coupon for a free coke during that time, over 8,500,000 in total. Their sales increased and in turn built them into the global brand they are today, all by using little pieces of paper. The power of coupons - eh?

Then in 1909 a cereal brand released some coupons, people went nuts for it. The cereal brand increased their sales by 500%, so at that point; every company cottoned on and started issuing coupons to sell more. This has continued to work until the present day. It is possible nowadays for people to take advantage of these coupons that companies release, and reduce your shopping bill to zero. By stacking your coupons and using them with sales or other offers, you can coupon your way to cheap or even free food. Love or hate Coca Cola, I'm very happy they invented coupons and it's as lucrative as it is now. Ironically they are one of the most stingy companies to issue coupons nowadays. You rarely see any money off, probably because they are now a globally recognised brand.

When most people think of coupons they think of their Nan in the Co-op in the seventies, do you remember green shield stamps? I certainly don't! My mum would always talk about her parents sticking them in a collection book until they'd saved enough of them. Just because the idea of coupons is old-fashioned, doesn't mean that they can't be used today. In fact, couponing and saving money is on trend once again. If they save you money, then why not use them?

Some coupons back in the old days had no expiration date and could be passed down through the family. Obviously times have changed, but one thing that's for sure, is that they are not going anywhere. Coupons can be found everywhere, and will continue to be around for all of our lifetimes. Don't be surprised if you see a 5 year old hand over a coupon for a free chocolate bar in the future!

Where do I find coupons?

Now that my history lesson is done, let me take off my glasses and get to the juicy stuff. Coupons are everywhere, and come in all different shapes and sizes. When people ask me "where is the best place to get coupons from?" There isn't a straightforward answer. They are scattered all over with several techniques to getting them. You can follow every method and be an extreme couponer, or just select the few that suit you and your lifestyle, and still save a very healthy amount!

With each method, as mentioned before, I've included some realistic goals for you. Follow all of them, and you could make a combined savings over £1,000 throughout the year. There is a tally to show you how quickly it all adds up, from just a few simple changes to the way you shop now.

Okay, I've done enough waffling. Let's get into it:

Online Coupons

When it comes to couponing in the UK, online is the place to be. It's the first place that I looked when I started my couponing journey 6 years ago, and it has only grown from there.

Imagine clicking a button and a piece of paper magically appearing that entitles you to a free pizza. Well stop imagining – because it's a reality. Often brands will offer coupons for free products or high value off for you to print out and take to the supermarket.

At least once a month, you can find coupons for free products – literally no spend. Simply take the coupon in, pick up the product, hand over the coupon and walk away – as simple as that! Quite often you will also find coupons with a high value off (such as £1 off a pack of butter), which can turn into a freebie if you wait for the product to go on sale, and use the coupon on top (full explanation on that later).

If you look in the right places, these coupons can be found all over the web, but most commonly you'd find them on brand websites, dedicated coupon pages and social media.

There are several dedicated coupon websites that have coupons for you to print out right away. To print most of these out you need to download a piece of software called "Coupon Printer.exe". It is used to keep the coupon trackable and to print the unique barcodes. Rest assured, it is not spam and you can print off every coupon on the web once it's downloaded, you won't need to reinstall.

Because of this, you are going to need a computer or laptop handy and a printer to print them off. Unfortunately you can't print off coupons from your smartphone or tablet just yet, because of the special coupon software (perhaps my next business venture?).

There are also several websites, forums and Facebook pages that are constantly being updated with coupons from around the web. I've listed my favourites to keep an eye on in the 'resources' section at the back of this book.

Without further ado, here are the websites to print off over £100s worth of coupons right now.

Dedicated coupon websites

SuperSavvyMe.co.uk

SuperSavvyMe is a P&G owned website containing coupons from their biggest brands. These normally include shampoos, feminine products, pet food and cleaning products. This website will not give you money off any food, unless cat food floats your boat!

At the time of writing, there are currently 25 coupons available to print off worth £18.75. It's likely you won't be using every single coupon they have listed, as you may not be rushing to use a coupon for feminine products if you are a man, and won't be buying pet food for an imaginary pet!

That being said, there are big brands offering coupons for products that a lot of households would use, such as Fairy, Bold, Flash and Head & Shoulders to name a few. You can print off each coupon once a month too to maximise your saving!

The coupons can be redeemed in any major supermarket unless they state otherwise. Also, be sure to check out the coupon terms and conditions when redeeming.

To print off the coupons you have to set up an account. From there simply add the coupons you want to print to your basket. Once you have picked the ones you want to print, hit the print button. Simple as that!

Once you have made an account, they send you emails when there are new coupons online. You can also sign up for free samples sent in the post too. Happy days!

If you didn't want to print your coupons, you can redeem SuperSavvyMe offers both online and in store with its new cashback option. Once you have selected which coupons you want to redeem, simply buy the items the coupons advertise and snap a picture of your receipt with that purchase on. You'll get the coupon's value as cashback applied to your account, which can be withdrawn through PayPal after you've earned £5.

Tip: You cannot redeem the same offer both as a printed coupon and as a cashback offer. You need to decide whether to print or use use cashback before you buy.

Achievable goal: Save £60 a year

Print off 5 coupons each month worth £5 in value (which you could achieve in one shop). That would save you £60 a year – and you have the potential to save a lot more than that.

Combined yearly savings: £60

Victoria.co.uk

Victoria is another P&G owned website that has a variety of coupons for their top brands. They have different offers to those found on SuperSavvyMe, as well as a few that are the same (but you can print them again from here). They also regularly offer free samples for you to claim which are mailed to you.

At the time of writing, there are currently 10 coupons available to print off worth £8.25, and six free samples to claim. Some exclusive coupons not found on SuperSavvyMe include Fixodent, Oral B and Lenor, along with some duplicates from brands such as Head and Shoulders and Flash (but there is nothing wrong with stocking up if you have two coupons!).

The coupons work in the same way as those from SuperSavvyMe and rotate frequently, so it's worth checking back to see what new ones they have. There isn't as many to choose from, but the brands are usually quite popular, so you might find something you need.

Achievable goal: Save £36 a year

Print off 3 coupons each month worth £3 in value (which you could do in one shop). That would save you £36 a year.

Combined yearly savings: £96

CaringEveryday.co.uk

Caring Everyday is a coupon site owned by Johnson & Johnson whose offers alternate on average once every month.

At time of writing, there are currently 35 coupons available to print off worth £49. The products are not as widely bought as the ones you'd find on SuperSavvyMe, however there are still savings to be made. At the moment you can find coupons for medications such as Sudafed, Calpol and Imodium, beauty products from Neutrogena and even hair regrowth foam from Regain. So unless you are a bald man suffering with heartburn and dry skin, you may not use most of them!

The coupons do rotate monthly, and it's not uncommon to find coupons for Johnson's baby products such as wipes, nappy creams and baby bath that are useful for parents. You may only print each offer once, but most months they refresh the offer or slightly change it to a different sized product, so you should be able to print something every month. Considering the selection of strange products on offer, there won't be as much to be saved from this website as some of the others, but it's still worth checking each month.

Printing them works the same way, sign up to Caring Everyday and select the coupons that you want to print. If you wanted to go crazy you could click the 'select all' button and print them all.

Achievable goal: Save £36 a year

Print off 3 coupons each month worth £3 in value (which you could do in one shop). That would save you £36 a year.

Combined yearly savings: £132

Coupon aggregates

MoneySavingExpert.com

Totally not biased at all (as they happen to be my employer!). MoneySavingExpert has a coupons page linking to coupons scattered around the web, and not on the sites above. This saves you the trouble of scouring websites and forums to try and find them yourself. Simply click through, print, and off you go.

Coupons found on here can really vary, but if you want some for your food shop – this is where you find them. Recently there has been coupons for totally free pizza, tuna, milk and more – just for printing out a piece of paper.

Coupons from this page can seriously add up. Right now there are over 100 coupons listed worth over £100 for you to print, which includes many top brands. Of course, you likely won't use all 100 of them, as there may be a lot of brands on here you don't buy... but as new coupons are added weekly, it'll be pretty soon before there is something new to print off.

Top brands such as Ristorante pizza, John West and Weetabix are regularly featured, so you can often find coupons for brands that are widely bought.

Achievable goal: Save £120 a year

Print off 15 coupons each month worth £10 in value (which you could do in one shop). That would save you £120 a year. With the amount of coupons on here, and constant new ones popping up, this figure could be a lot more!

Combined yearly savings: £252

Those are the main places online to check and print out coupons. By following and keeping an eye on those websites, you'll be up to date on all the latest coupons so that you never miss a deal. Some coupons can be very short lived - especially if they are coupons for freebie products with limited availability. Quite often you will see coupon promotions for a 'Free Goodfellas Pizza' with only 10,000 redemptions available. As a young and pizza addicted lad - it's offers like this I can't miss out on!

Even if you stop at online coupons, you could already be saving £252 a year on things that you normally buy, and you wouldn't be going 'extreme'. Yes, by doing online couponing you may occur some costs such as ink and paper, or even a printer if you don't have one, but the money saved will pay for that ten times over. But why stop there? There are plenty more ways to get your hands on coupons and save money ahead...

Contacting manufacturers

Do you want to get high value exclusive coupons that no one else has their hands on? I'm talking free products, £5 off, £10 off... the sky is the limit. Contacting manufacturers is the way to go. This is one of the best ways to get coupons, and all it could take is a simple email.

Major food companies cannot survive without consumer feedback, both good and bad. If they had none at all, they would have no way of improving. If you have something wrong with them, they get some information to improve and 9 times out of 10 you will be reimbursed either in coupons or free products sent to your house. Also on the flip side, if you love what they are doing and their products, sending feedback could result in coupons and freebies as well.

The most cost and time effective way to get in touch with a brand is Googling their website and filling out a 'contact us' form with your concerns or praise. Here are some tips on doing both to score some high value manufacturer coupons:

Complaining

We live in Great Britain, but one thing Britain is not so great at, is voicing our opinions. Has your food ever not been up to standard in a restaurant and you didn't say anything? Has one of your packets of crisps ever been stuck to the outer packaging, leaving the crisps all stale and horrible? (A common complaint by the way). Well, you should never stay quiet about it. If you have paid money for something, it's not unreasonable to expect it to be in full working order – even when it comes to that one stale packet of crisps!

Lots of people don't speak out for fear of insulting or fear of speaking out itself, but think of all the products you've bought that have gone wrong recently. How much did you collectively pay?

Quite often if people are lamenting to me that a product has gone wrong, the usual response to the question "did you complain?" is "no, I can't be bothered." Let's say on average, one product a month that you buy from the supermarket has something wrong with it that is worth complaining about. For each complaint you make, they send you £5 worth of coupons or replacement products - that's £60 per year. That should be something worth getting bothered about in my eyes!

The fact of the matter is, nothing can be done if nothing is said, and this is the way to start being repaid when things don't go right. If something is not right in a restaurant, let them know! If you find a nail in your cereal, don't keep quiet! It can seriously add up, and you get a better level of service.

No complaint is too small. I've complained for some silly things (yet still valid complaints) and got a big return from them. Quite often more in value than what the original product costs. This is where a lot of my freebies and high value shopping hauls have come from.

One of my favourite examples, is when I got a pack of celebrations for Christmas from one of my relatives. I was super excited to tuck in and eat them, but imagine my horror when I found out there was only one Malteaser chocolate in the whole tub. That could've started a civil war in my household! I was not having this, so sent an email to Mars to complain. Three days later, I had a reply saying they were sending me vouchers to apologise and soon after, I had £5 worth of chocolate vouchers in my hand. All from sending a simple email. I bought as many Malteasers as the voucher could buy me – to avoid an internal conflict!

If you thought THAT was extreme, I can probably top it... Yes, I have been known to weigh products to see if it was the correct weight, and measuring them to see if it was the right size. You'd be surprised how many fall short. On one occasion, one of my blocks of butter said it weighed 250g on the packaging... but after placing it on my scales - THE HORROR - it was 247g! Another email went off to say it was underweight along with the packaging codes, and a week later, I had a coupon for £3 off any product in their range on my doormat. And the best part? I didn't even pay for that butter in the first place because I had a coupon!

You don't have to go as far as I have, however if you have complaints about your products, then you shouldn't sit quiet. There is a lot of money to be had by voicing your opinion. You won't be moaning as when you purchase products, you as a buyer expect them to work as advertised, and if it doesn't, then that's worthy of complaint!

If complaining is not your thing, then you could try sending off emails with suggestions instead. For example if you don't like a brand's new packaging and think it'd be better in another colour, or if you don't like the new flavour and send off some suggestions which could help them improve in the future, sometimes they appreciate this and send you coupons too.

Achievable goal: Save £60 a year

You must have at least one thing to complain about a month, for when things don't go as planned or work as expected. Send off a quick email when it does and receive £5 worth of coupons each time - you'd save £60 a year.

Combined yearly savings: £312

Complimenting

Strap yourself in, because this is a lucrative (and also one of my favourite ways) to get high value coupons – and have a bit of fun in the process. On the flip side to everything I've just said, another great way to get high value coupons, is by complimenting your favourite brands.

Just like when complaining, companies love to hear from their customers, so if you really love a brand of cereal that you eat every day, why not send them a nice email to tell them that? If they are in a good mood, then you might get rewarded as a thank you.

Just by sending off a quick email to brands, I've received £100s worth of coupons and free products through the post for minimal effort. It's like Christmas opening them up to see what they send you.

The unfortunate thing is, that you're not as likely to get coupons this way, as big brands receive 100s of emails each day and it all depends on what kind of mood the person looking at your email is in. There are however ways to increase your chances of success. This is by making your email stand out – and do something different to grab their attention.

If you create something new and shareable for them, then they can use it as content for their social media channels, marketing or in future campaigns. In return, they would send you vouchers as a way to compensate. It doesn't have to be much either, a small poem or drawing could do the trick. Just with that tiny bit of effort, it will drastically increase your chances. Here are some ideas that I've tried out:

Send them a poem

If you are a budding wordsmith like me, one of my favourite methods to spice up a complimentary email is to write a poem about their brand. I actually did an experiment by sending 45 companies the same poem to see what kind of response I got. 19 replied and sent me £75+ worth of coupons and free products. Copying and pasting the same email to each company and tweaking them slightly only took me a few hours over a weekend – and got me a very nice return!

I'd recommend creating a poem that features the company name and their brand to make it personalised. In my poems, I just change a few words each time when sending to each brand to personalise it to them, and it seems to work. My regular go-to looks like this:

(Company name), (Company name) you are a dream,
No other (drink/snack) could be so supreme,
Oozing with joy and bursting with flavour,
With every (sip/bite) you are my saviour.

I sounded barking mad to my mother who was sat next to me when I was coming up with this poem…! This little beauty however got me £20 worth of coupons in the post from Innocent drinks, £15 worth of freebies from Jordan's cereal and £10 from Purina cat food.

Send them a drawing

If you have children or grandchildren who want something to do, get them to draw a picture of their favourite food and send it off to the brand. Not only will that tug on their heart strings, it should keep your pockets full in the process.

Create a song for them

If you're a talented musician, why not create a short song or replace lyrics of a popular song with your favourite brand – and send it to them. With this method, sending through email might be tricky due to spam filters – so try sending it to them through social media, either directly or through private message (if you don't want your friends to watch you sing about Rice Krispies…)

Send them a birthday card

And finally, birthday cards are another great way to attract attention. If you Google your favourite brands, or look up their Wikipedia page, you should be able to see when they were founded. If it's a big birthday, brands might advertise on social media or TV as well, which gives you more of a chance. You can pick up a cheap 29p card from high street card shops, and the return you make will be a lot more. Remember to use 2nd class post to reduce costs too.

I once got sent £20 worth of coupons for seeing an advertisement on TV that it was a brand's birthday and sending a cheap card to their business address. Obviously this one will cost you money to send out with the card and stamp, but it gives you a good shot at standing out. Remember to put your return address on the card/envelope though if you want coupons back!

Hopefully by putting in the extra effort, you'll stand a good chance at getting some freebies. Here are some extra do's and don'ts to maximise your success:

DO - finish off your email with a nice line to prompt them that you'd like to try more of their products. I always finish by saying *"I must try your new XXX range that I keep seeing – they look yummy! Need to add it to my shopping list."* In a lot of cases it prompts the reply that they'll send you some. Just adding this one line into an email once got me a massive £50 package full of food shipped to my house to try a new range from Amy's Kitchen.

DON'T – just ask straight away for coupons to be sent to you. On the whole this doesn't work very well. It's better to actually give the brand something – and hope to receive coupons in return. Even if the thing you are giving them is as small as a compliment.

If a company replies to your email with just a generic thank you and doesn't offer any freebies or coupons, THEN would be the best time to ask, as you have started a conversation with someone in the marketing team. By replying to their email saying *"Thank you for the response. I'm very keen to try any new products and your xxx product I keep seeing. If you ever have any free samples or coupons available in exchange for feedback, please do let me know."* This doesn't always work, but it might prompt them to send you something if they are feeling nice.

DO – be sure to check your spelling and grammar, especially of the companies name. Don't make the same mistake I have done several times in the past by completely misspelling the brand name – as it doesn't look good. If you are sending multiple emails off to different companies too, be sure that you have the right grammar and information in relation to that product if you are copying and pasting the same message. The last thing you'd want is to send an email about how much you enjoy eating their food to a feminine hygiene product brand… totally didn't happen to me…!

DON'T – go purely for massive brands such as Cadbury, Mars and P&G. In my experience, the bigger the brand and more products they look after, the less likely you are to get coupons. The most success comes from individually owned companies or small brands that don't have 100s of people working for them. I've included a list below of the companies I've had constant success with in the past, and most of them are privately owned.

DO – be patient when waiting for replies. Some companies get hundreds of emails a day, so could take a while before they get to yours. Usually they will tell you in their first correspondence with you if they are sending you coupons or freebies. If you get a generic response such as "we'll pass your comments on to the marketing team", then unfortunately it means you won't be sent anything (unless you follow up and persuade them!).

Brands worth contacting

I've been writing to companies since I started couponing and have had constant success with a few brands, so hopefully you can too. When emailing these brands, I have mostly used poems in order to increase my chances and they have resulted in something back, so be sure to try them out. Try out other smaller companies too to see if you get lucky!

- Innocent drinks
- Purina cat/dog food
- Pataks
- Blue Dragon
- Jordan's cereals
- Pilgrims Choice
- Arm & Hammer
- Saucy Fish Co
- Little Dish
- Vita Coco

Achievable goal: Save £120 a year

Email 5-10 different companies a month, maybe a couple each weekend. If only two come back each month and send you freebies or vouchers of £5 value each, you'd be saving £120 a year.

Combined yearly savings: £432

Magazine coupons

You want coupons in magazines? I'll give you coupons in magazines. Actually, no… paws off… they are my coupons!

You can find coupons and freebies in magazines every single month, in a variety of different prints. Some of the best magazines for coupons are free to pick up, which is great for us couponers as it means no unnecessary spending. There are also monthly freebies that you might see in premium magazines such as free beauty products, but again, it's worth weighing up cost.

Some of these magazine coupons can be quite lucrative! Quite a few times I've found myself picking up 10 copies of a magazine (the free ones of course), as it had a coupon in for a free 1.5L bottle of Coca Cola. Absolutely no effort required, just rip it out of the page and hand it over at the till. I've seen coupons for free tea, milk and even a coupon for £1 off butter, which was reduced to £1 - which made THAT free as well. You can see how this gets addictive don't you? Here are the best places to pick them up:

In store supermarket magazines

This right here is your holy grail. In the monthly magazines from big wigs such as Tesco, Sainsbury's and even Boots, there are usually pages of coupons for you to use. The coupons rotate with each issue and include different products every month. The best part - both the Tesco and Boots magazine are free to pick up.

Tesco Magazine

Every month, Tesco releases a new in store magazine with coupons inside the first page. There are also sometimes hidden coupons for various brands spread out within the magazine, so it's also worth having a flick through.

Some of these coupons can be very juicy indeed! As Tesco is my preferred supermarket, I've saved £100s over the years by using them. They aren't paying me to say that (although I wish they were!). My favourite coupon, despite all the freebies they offer, probably has to be when they had 50p off any Maggi spice product. It may not be the most exciting product to have a coupon on, but trust me - it was! The spice mixes where priced at £1, but were also on a 3 for 2 offer. I was able to use a coupon on each product I bought, so for every three bought, I got £1.50 off with my coupons… and at the till, one of them scanned in for free, which knocked another £1 off. This made every three that I bought only 50p (around 16.6p per pack!). I did buy quite a few! Could practically bathe in Sticky BBQ Chicken!

There have been some freebie coupons in the Tesco magazine in the past, and usually every month contains around £5 to £10 worth of coupons inside. Most of the time it's for money off big brands too, which means you can use them alongside what you are buying things in your weekly shop.

Alongside money off coupons, you might find 'extra Clubcard points' offers if you buy specific products. These are only worth using if you're going to buy that product anyway as the value of Clubcard points are very low. One point is the equivalent of 1p in value, so if you are buying a £2 product to get 50 extra Clubcard points, it means you'd be £1.50 out of pocket.

A cool thing about these magazine coupons, is if you're an online shopper they have discount codes on each one, which you can enter online to get money off of your shopping. So if there is a coupon for £1 off cheese, you can either cut out the coupon and use it in store, or enter the code online.

The magazine switches over at the beginning of the month and the coupons within usually last for around 30 days.

> *Tip: As the Tesco magazine is free… you can pick up as many as you want (within reason). If you think you'll use more than one coupon in a month, pick up a stack of magazines to tide you over.*

Achievable goal: Save £52 a year

If you're a regular Tesco shopper, just using one £1 off coupon from the magazine with your weekly shop can add up to £52 in yearly savings. There is the potential to save a lot more though.

Combined yearly savings: £484

Boots Magazine

The Boots magazine is similar to Tesco, having a page of coupons in the back for both money off and bonus point offers when you buy certain products. The magazine itself costs £1 (or you get one copy free if you have a Boots Advantage card). So unfortunately with this one, you can't pick up a stack full.

Coupons found here are usually for various toiletries, healthcare and beauty products, some of which makes you a nice saving. Boots are notorious for having high prices on their toiletries however. Big name brands of shampoo, body wash and toothpaste can normally be found cheaper in the supermarkets, so be sure (even if there is a coupon for them at Boots), that you are getting the cheapest price.

Don't be so quick to discard the bonus point offers with this one though. Some of them can be quite lucrative thanks to the high value of Advantage points. I once spotted a deal where a coupon from the magazine actually made you 50p 'profit' (in points) for using it. You received an extra 200 Advantage points (worth £2) if you bought any two shampoos in the store… and this included the cheapest ones on the shelf! So if you picked up two of the cheapest Boots own brand shampoo at 75p each, you'd only pay £1.50, and the 200 extra points would mean you were 50p in profit. Always worth looking out for.

Achievable goal: Save £12 a year

Just using one £1 off coupon a month (or a 100 extra points coupon if you were buying the product anyway), would add up to £12 a year in savings.

Combined yearly savings: £496

Sainsbury's Magazine

The Sainsbury's magazine is a little different. They have coupons in it every month, however it costs £1.60. In order to make use of the magazine, the coupons you're using must be worth £1.60… and that's just to break even. When it comes to this one, only buy it if you want it OR the coupons are all for something you use. If you buy the magazine for the coupons and don't use them, then you aren't saving money. There may be value in this for Sainsbury's shoppers, but I would personally avoid this one.

Other Magazines

When it comes to other magazines, they are hit and miss. Other supermarkets may issue magazines, but whether they have coupons in vary every month (though it's worth checking).

Occasionally you might see a coupon in 'Red' or 'Woman's Own', and it should be well advertised on their front cover if they do. So it's worth having a glance every month to see if they have something. Remember, that some of these magazines can cost £2,3,4 or £5+, so be sure to work out if you are getting value from it.

It's not only worth checking the front cover for coupons, but also the freebies you get with them. Some magazines give away £12 mascara, nail varnish or eye-liner for free when you buy them. If you are spending £2 to get a £10+ product, then that's a pretty good deal (if you'll use it). I luckily don't need make-up with my free flawless skin!

Achievable goal: Save £20 a year

Ladies (or gents), grabbing a Mascara freebie twice a year from a magazine and saving £10 on the retail price can save £20 a year – and have a magazine to read.

Combined yearly savings: £516

Newspaper coupons

For those of you that have seen the sheer scale of couponing in the US from the TV show 'Extreme Couponing', you will know that coupons are all over their newspapers.

Unfortunately the same cannot be said here. It isn't unheard of to find coupons in the papers but it is not as common. Luckily for us, the best coupons can be found in newspapers that are free to pick up (but more on that later).

There have been some great examples of coupons in the newspapers here in the UK. Back in 2014, Morrisons released a coupon several times for £5 off fruit and veg with no minimum spend when you bought The Sun. The paper only cost you 40p and you got £5 worth of fresh fruit & veg for free.

You may be thinking "Why would they do that?" This would be a marketing ploy to get people into store and spend more on other items while they buy the fruit & veg. Us savvy couponers didn't fall for it though... we got as much fruit & veg as we could stomach!

People went crazy for this deal, and rightly so! I ended up getting £20 worth of fruit & veg for my mum and I, which we only paid £1.60 for (the price of 4 newspapers). Other couponers with larger families got a whole lot more. Please be wary of food wastage with offers like this however.

Here are the Newspaper coupons to be looking out for:

Metro Newspaper

The best place to find coupons in newspapers is The Metro, and luckily for us couponers, it's free to pick up. You'll usually find these papers at train and bus stations and around public transport. If you are a London commuter like me, you'd be use to the mass of discarded Metro papers around every station and tube train.

While it's the best Newspaper to get coupons in, it can be hit and miss. For the big coupon promotions, it will usually be plastered on the front cover of the newspaper, making it easy to spot. For most others, they may be hidden away deep into the paper and not advertised elsewhere.

If you are a commuter like me, it's worth having a flick through on the tube or train every day to see if there is something in there. More often than not, there won't be, but it's always worth checking.

Within the Metro newspaper, there are three main types of coupons that will crop up. These include fast food vouchers, £5 off £40 spends at Lidl and the elusive 'freebie' coupons.

Fast Food Coupons

The most common type of coupon in the Metro is the fast food discount coupons. This includes McDonald's meals for £1.99 and Burger King meal deals. You'll see these several times a week or even daily just by flicking through, and you can easily end up with a pocket full of them if you keep ripping them out each day. It's worth taking just one strip of vouchers with you, if you think you might end up at a McDonalds or Burger King in the near future. The coupons usually have long expiry dates, so you can hold onto it for a while.

A normal McDonald's meal without the voucher would set you back £4.49 for a burger, chips and drink... but the vouchers get you a burger and fries for £1.99. If you wanted to add a drink too, you'd get the full whack for £2.98 - which saves you £1.51 on your meal (or 30%). It may not sound like much, but the pennies add up. If you have a family of four, and all used a voucher (which you are allowed to do), it'd cost you £11.92 instead of £17.96. Do that once a month, and that's over £70 a year. So it may not seem like a huge saving at the time, but it's still worth it.

Achievable goal: Save £18 a year

Keep some of these coupons in your bag or coat pocket at all times in case you happen to visit a fast food chain. Use one a month you would be saving £18 a year. If you use them for several people in your family, it could save you a lot more!

Combined yearly savings: £534

£5 off £40 Lidl spend coupons

The second most common coupon you'd see in the Metro are £5 off £40 spend coupons for Lidl. These are usually plastered over the front page, so you should know when one of these are in the paper. They usually last for around a week after the day the paper was printed, and are valid around the country.

A lot of people say they struggle to spend more than £40 on their weekly shop at Lidl, but if you think you're going to spend £80+, you can pick up two papers and use them both. They usually come with the term "one coupon per transaction".

Tip: this can be avoided by splitting your basket into two, and using a coupon for each transaction (which is totally fine to do). Keep an eye on front pages each day for this one to crop up.

If you live near a Lidl, then this could come in very handy. They appear around once a month, so if you aren't loyal to one supermarket, or Lidl is your supermarket of choice, then you can make some decent savings with this. Just remember, don't go spending over the odds just to use the coupon. If you think you're going to spend £25, adding another £15 worth of shopping means you are spending £10 more than you would have done after the coupon has been used.

Achievable goal: Save £30 a year

Use one of these coupons every other month when the coupons roll round, and you'd save £30 a year.

Combined yearly savings: £564

Freebie coupons

And finally, one of the least common (but great when they come around) are the freebie coupons. Around once a month you might see a coupon for a free product in the Metro. There have been coupons for free Kingsmill Thins, Weetabix drinks and more in the past. Most of the time it's in line with a new product campaign, and incentivises people to try it out. If you aren't spending anything, you should be more than happy to oblige!

If you manage to spot one of these... remember, these newspapers are free. There is nothing stopping you picking two... three... ten... or how ever many newspapers you'd like with the voucher in. Just don't be 'that guy' who clears the shelf of papers so no one else can read them! Remember to check the T&Cs of the freebie coupon to see whether you can use more than one in one go.

There are lots of coupon Facebook pages and groups who are normally the first to post when things like this come around. I have included a list of pages to follow in the 'resources' section at the back of this book. It's worth following them to make sure you don't miss these coupons.

Achievable goal: Save £24 a year

Get your hands on one of these freebie coupons a month worth £2 in value, and you'd save £24 a year.

Combined yearly savings: £588

Other Newspapers

When it comes to the other paid for newspapers, it's quite rare to find coupons inside. When mainstream papers have a coupon inside, it is usually advertised quite well on the front page, as it is usually a marketing ploy to get you to buy the paper. As much as we want there to be pages and pages of coupons (like they do in Sunday papers in the US), coupons that you'd find here are for low value items such as a "Free Chocolate Bar at McColl's when you buy the Daily Mirror".

The thing to watch out for with these, as quite a lot of the time, the paper costs nearly the same as the freebie! If you buy the paper to get the free chocolate bar, but have spent 40p to get it, then your saving is going to be minimal. It's always good to ask yourself "do I need it?" before splashing out any cash to get these coupons.

You may also occasionally find token collection offers in the mainstream papers such as The Sun and Daily Mail. These work so that if you buy a certain number of papers, you can send off your tokens in exchange for vouchers, gift cards or the more famous £9.50 holidays. Again, these are not as they seem.

There was a promotion once in the Sun, where if you collected 10 tokens in papers over a two week period, you would be sent a £5 Morrison's gift card. Sounds good on the surface right? When you looked into it further, the cost of 10 papers and the postage to get your freebie added up to over £8, meaning by completing the offer, you'd be over £3 out of pocket!

Similarly with the "£9.50 holidays", after all things are done and paid for, it will likely cost you triple that in total to claim the offer. The £9.50 that they advertise is how much you pay towards the holiday. What they don't mention is the 20 papers at 40p each (£8), postage (£1) and fees for booking a caravan site (up to £10). So be careful to add up the costs with these offers to make sure you know what you're paying (and if it's worth it!).

So for the other papers, keep an eye on the front pages to see if there are any coupons inside. If you see something that you would use (and it's still good value after the cost of your paper) then it might be worth it. You may see one offer or so a month for you to take up.

Achievable goal: Save £12 a year

Keep an eye out and use one coupon a month worth £1 in value after newspaper costs, and you'd save £12 a year.

Combined yearly savings: £600

Supermarket loyalty schemes

Being signed up to supermarket loyalty schemes has its benefits, mainly because you get coupons from them. There are many to sign up to that give you rewards for spending and coupons that encourage you to spend (but don't fall into that trap!).

My personal recommendation is to sign up to every loyalty card you can find for brands that you buy from. Will it take time? It might, but the amount you get in return should be worth it. Will it give you more emails and post? Probably, but that's why you get a new email address. What we are after are the rewards. Most loyalty schemes give you rewards even if you aren't spending in their store. They might be trying to get you to buy things but if you actually need something from there, you are quids in.

One time, I had my eye on a really great gift set as a birthday present for my friend. The price was £14.99… yuk! It was near impossible to get any other type of discount for it apart from having a coupon sent to me as part of my loyalty schemes.

I waited till the last week to see if a coupon was sent to me, to make it cheaper. Risky, I know! I was just about to give up and then BAM, £5 off £15 spend came in the post. Jordon 1 – The System 0! Let's keep a tally of how many times I beat the system and got a discount… Hope you don't get bored after the first 1,000!

So what loyalty cards are the best you might be wondering? I could be here all day and list them all, but here are my top picks based on rewards and points accumulated through spending.

Tesco Clubcard

Receive one point per pound spent on groceries as well as points in many other stores and companies like insurance, Tesco Bank and Esso Fuel.

Not only do they give you rewards per pound you spend, but you also receive money saving coupons nearly every month through the post. You regularly receive £5 off £40 spend coupons known as 'Helping Hand Coupons', and can get books of these lasting you the next 6 weeks with £5 off each week. If you can combine those with your coupon shopping too, you are really in the money.

You also receive money saving coupons in the post on items tailored to what you have been buying in their supermarket. If you buy cat food every time you visit, more likely than not you will get coupons for money off cat food. One of the systems that Tesco has in place so that you save money on the things you need (or to go back into their store to buy it, whichever way you look at it). Like always, there will be things that you might not want, so don't fall into the trap just because you have a coupon, unless it's a great deal and you want to give it a try.

The actual loyalty aspect of the card is one of the strongest in terms of value, but only if you claim certain rewards. For every 500 points you collect, you earn £5 worth of rewards, which can be doubled or tripled up when redeeming on selected offers. You can choose to spend your Clubcard vouchers in store, but the real value in these lie in the 'up to triple' you get online on selected offers..

Some of the best exchanges are for restaurant vouchers (usually £2.50 of Clubcard for £5 of restaurant vouchers), Airmiles (£2.50 of Clubcard for 500-625 miles), days out and many more options. It's always worth having a look when you have accrued enough points to see what offer is best for you, but definitely take advantage of the double or triple value if possible.

They also have a program that allows you to save up all of your points through the year and get your rewards in November to spend over Christmas. It makes the festive period cheaper for a lot of people.

Tip: Be sure to check your Tesco Clubcard account to see if you have any rewards unclaimed. The points you accumulate go back to since you started your account, so you might have the odd £5 lying in wait in your account to be spent, that you totally forgot about. You get a Clubcard statement quarterly with all of your earnings, but it only shows you earnings for that quarter, so it's always worth a check if there are vouchers in there from a year ago that you forgot to use.

Achievable goal: Save £94 a year

There is quite a lot going on with Tesco Clubcard, so let's break it down a little to get our goals:

Collect 1,000 Clubcard points throughout the year through spending and extra point coupons to get £10 in Clubcard points (which can be exchanged for up to £40 of vouchers).

Use a 'helping hand' coupon for £5 off your weekly shop every other month (or when they send them) to save £30 a year.

Use two coupons a month from the targeted coupons they send you of products you normally buy to save £2 a month or £24 throughout the year.

Those three little bonuses from being signed up to Clubcard will net you an extra £94 in yearly savings.

Combined yearly savings: £694

Sainsbury's Nectar Card

Much like Tesco Clubcard, you can use a Nectar card to collect points at a range of places including Sainsbury's, BP, Expedia, eBay, British Gas and more. The amount of points you receive per pound spent varies, however shopping in store at Sainsbury's will get you one point for every £1 spent. Unfortunately with Nectar, you'll have to collect 2 points to get 1p in value, so you'll need to spend and collect more to make rewards from it.

Redemptions on Nectar points are not as strong as they are with Tesco Clubcard, partly due to the lower value in points. Much like Tesco, you are able to double or triple your points with rewards online, and this is the best place to go when it comes to redeeming. Using points as in store credit gives very poor value, giving you £2.50 off your shop for every 500 points.

Deals that you can get on redeeming your Nectar points for double or triple value can change. That being said, the offers I have used Nectar points on (which seem to stick around) include 500 points for £3.75 worth of Pizza Express vouchers and 500 points for £5 off at Merlin Attractions. It's worth noting that you get a higher value at Pizza Express with Tesco Clubcard (250 points = £5 in vouchers), but this is the best offers that Nectar has available.

Aside from the loyalty aspect of the card, it's rare that Sainsbury's offer any other types of coupons with Nectar. They may occasionally send out some coupons in the post (though that is a thing of the past), and you may see coupons printed out at the till linked to your Nectar Card when shopping, but that is unfortunately as far as it gets. Here's hoping that changes!

Achievable goal: Save £10 a year

There isn't as much value to be had with Nectar, and they don't offer coupons to get extra points very often, so collecting 1000 points a year worth £5 (which can be doubled to £10 on their online offers) is realistic.

Combined yearly savings: £704

Boots Advantage Card

This is actually one of the most generous loyalty schemes out there, due to both the high point per pound spent, and the extra point promotions they have. While Boots isn't great for buying all of your weekly shopping, it can certainly save you a lot of money if you are a regular shopper.

For every £1 that you spend in store, you get 4 points back onto your card. Points are valued at 1p each, so to get 500 points (£5), you'd have to spend £125 in store, or take part in bonus point offers, which come around quite often. It is the best value loyalty card per pound spent of all supermarkets.

Around once a month when signed up for Boots Advantage, you'll get some coupons in the post for money off or extra points coupons along with a summary of what you have earned so far. Quite often you can find some good coupons in here, and like Tesco, it is targeted to what you would usually buy.

You can also find great bonus offers such as 1,000 extra points when you spend £50 in store. These are very lucrative offers as you are essentially paying £40 for £50 worth of goods, which is a good discount if you were going to buy something anyway. You can either get an extra £10 worth of goodies there and then or stash your points away for a later date (which could be invaluable when Christmas gift buying season rolls around).

Tip: If you see one of these offers and you think you are going to spend more than the £50, it's worth dividing up your basket. You can use the offer as many times as you want on most occasions, so if you have 2 baskets both with £50 worth of items in, you will get £20 back in points from your £100 spend. A clever and easy way to get the most bang for your buck!

Do you remember the old Boots coupon machines they used to have in store? I loved these machines as a kid, and always used to ask my mum to put her card in and see what coupons she could print (I guess my obsession with coupons started earlier than I thought!). A lot of those machines are not around anymore, and instead have been replaced with the Boots App. If you download it, there are plenty of exclusive bonus point and coupon offers that you can link directly to your card, with no paper coupons needed.

Whether you are a regular Boots shopper or not, if you can target some of the high value extra point offers, your savings will add up. If you know that you need to buy an expensive razor or hairdryer that you've had your eye on for a while, by waiting until a high value point offer comes around, you could save a lot of cash over the year.

Achievable goal: Save £30 a year

Either grab yourself one of the high value bonus point offers a few times a year, or take advantage of the postal and mobile app offers. This can easily add up to £30 in savings over the year.

Combined yearly savings: £734

Morrison's More Card

The Morrison's More Card isn't worth jumping for joy over unfortunately. Unless you're a frequent Morrison's shopper, it will take you a while to build up enough points to get coupons from.

For every £1 you spend in store, or at a Morrison's petrol station, you get 5 points loaded to your card. Once you have accrued a total of 5,000 points (a spend of £1,000), you'll get a coupon automatically printed off at the till, giving you £5 off your next purchase at Morrison's with no minimum spend. The coupons last for just over a year, but if you do get your hands of one, using sooner rather than later is better in case you lose it. You don't want to spend £1,000 to then lose your only reward!

They do run special bonus point offers when buying selected products. Amounts of bonus points can vary from in the 100s up to 1,000 (which is £1 worth of points) so be sure to look out for them. If you are signed up to the Morrison's More Card, you may get some of these extra point coupons at the till too, so worth keeping an eye out.

With or without the bonus point offers, you'd still need to spend a lot in order to get your £5 off coupons. If you shop at Morrison's each week, you may be able to earn enough points for a £5 coupon once or twice a year, but if you don't shop regularly at Morrison's, I wouldn't be changing supermarkets to pounce on this loyalty card.

My Waitrose Card

This maybe my favourite loyalty card for one reason, and one reason alone… FREE TEA. Well it used to be free, now it's a single penny if you play your cards right.

In the past, Waitrose had an offer where you could walk into the supermarket with your Waitrose card and skip out on your merry way with a free hot drink, just by flashing your card at the till. Unfortunately, they stopped that so you have to make a purchase with your card in order to get the free cuppa. The loophole here is… there is no minimum spend. You could pick up a loose banana for around 10p… perhaps a loose carrot for around 8p… or even a single date for a measly penny. Pay for your loose fruit and ask for the free hot drink, and Bob's your uncle!

Other fun perks with the card include a free newspaper when you spend £5 in store, and the card also gives you the opportunity to 'pick your own offers', to get exclusive discounts off of certain products in store. This promotion has just recently been cut back however, meaning it's nothing worth getting excited over unfortunately.

Achievable goal: Save £18 a year

You don't even need to buy any shopping, just stop in for a singular date and a tea once a month and you'll be saving £18 a year… and have very happy tastebuds. Coffee is also available for a caffeine fix.

Combined yearly savings: £752

With the loyalty cards mentioned above, even if you shop around and don't regularly commit to one supermarket, the points can still add up over time if you make purchases there. Just for being signed up, the perks alone are the best things, from coupons to free tea.

Of the ones mentioned, you get the most value from Tesco Clubcard and Boots Advantage cards - and those are my personal favourites as they send you coupons randomly in the post!

Tip: if you don't want to be carrying all that extra plastic around with you in your wallet, there's an app on your phone which can do it for you. The app 'Stocard' can store all of these loyalty cards on your phone (and many other high street ones), so all you have to do is show the barcode on your phone to the cashier. It can be a real time saver – and it means you never forget them too!

On-product coupons

When you are out going wild in the aisles with your coupons - don't go too wild! Coupons can be anywhere – especially on products. They can be anything from a tag hanging off of a product to an all singing all dancing on pack promotion. What is the ultimate couponer's dream? Finding an on-product coupon... on a product you have a coupon for in the first place! THAT is the couponing jackpot!

So what should you be looking out for? Basically anything that stands out on the shelf. If it stands out, there might be an on-pack promotion attached to it. If you've ever looked at a box of cereal and thought "that's not the colour it normally is..." That is usually an on pack promotion. They range from coupons to competitions, and sometimes both. No matter what it is, it's worth having a look. This is the most way of finding coupons on products.

Tip: It goes without saying though, don't go spending money you weren't going to spend on products just to get a coupon – you'd just be spending unnecessarily.

If it does have just a competition, remember to read the small print. There was a promotion recently on Butterkist Popcorn to win a holiday. In the small print it said "every entry receives a 50p off coupon for your next purchase of Butterkist."

Another thing to look out for is hang tags on the products. If you see a little piece of paper around the neck of a bottle, be sure to read it. You might get rewarded with a coupon. Coupons like these that are on the outside of a product can be used straight away too.

'Try me free' offers are also great at getting free goodies, and these are only found in the supermarket. Most of them have big promotions on the product or shelf saying "Try Me Free." All you have to do to get your money back is send off the receipt of you buying the product, and they usually send you a check in the post with your money back.

Also look out for those "Love me or your money back" promotions. Us Brits do not like to complain, but in this case you must! If you find anything wrong with it or anyone in your family tries it and doesn't like it, tell them. You get your money back no questions asked.

There are other examples that you might have seen in the US such as peeling coupon stickers, blinker boxes and coupon machines. Unfortunately they are very rare here. I do however live in hope that one day there will be a £1 off coupon peelie stuck to a £1 product! Believe!

Achievable goal: Save £12 a year

Even if you don't spot many, finding only two 50p off coupons a month, would mean a £12 yearly saving.

Combined yearly savings: £764

Receipt coupons

The most boring pieces of paper (and the most frightening if you look at what you spent), just got a bit more fun. You can often find coupons either hidden or printed out as receipts both at the supermarket and in all walks of life.

These are called till spit coupons. Most of the ones you find in the supermarket are attached to your loyalty cards, so after you pay, you get coupons printed out at the till. They can range from money off certain products, £5 off your next shop offers (or online shop for Sainsbury's customers), to extra points coupons. These can add up to a lot of money off, however there are a few snags.

Most of these supermarket coupons printed at the till don't have very long lives on them. The average till spit coupon only lasts around a week. The main point is for the supermarket to entice you back for next weeks shop. If you were going to come back next week - then great, take advantage. If you weren't, it may not be worth the risk of getting 50p off your can of beans... as you may fill your basket up with a few other goodies that override the saving.

If you are signed up to Tesco Clubcard, they are the best for this kind of coupon. I regularly receive extra point and money off coupons at the till with my shopping (and they cleverly give you coupons for things that you normally buy, based on what products are regularly bought linked to that Clubcard).

Similarly, (straying away from supermarkets a little here) wherever you go in life, you should always check the bottom of your receipts.

Whether it's a high street retailer, or a restaurant, there are offers all over them!

Popular restaurants such as Frankie & Benny's, TGI Fridays, Harvester, KFC, Chiquitos and many more have 'free main meal', 'free desert' or a percentage off your next bill by filling out a short survey. Usually these coupons last for around a week to a month after you first eat there, so if you were looking to return, you could save some dough.

It's the same with some high street retailers. Check at the bottom of the receipts for any '20% off your next purchase' promotions to see if you can get money off next time. It's worth noting, a lot of receipts have surveys to win cash or vouchers for giving them your thoughts. These are best avoided, as your chances of winning are low, unless you are entered into the draw while claiming your freebie coupons of course!

Final little tip with these (though use your conscience on whether you want to do it or not). If you are eating at a restaurant, have a look outside before you go in for any discarded receipts. You can quickly fill out the survey on your phone and hey presto - you've got a coupon for when you eat there. Most of the time they just give you a code to write on the receipt, or send you an email, so you don't have to print anything. You would be leaving a review on someone else's meal, that you yourself didn't consume - so it's up to you to decide if that sits with you.

At my local restaurant complex, there is an Italian restaurant that I love to eat at, and luckily for me, printed on the back of all receipts for the Cineworld literally next door, is a coupon for 20% off that very restaurant! This one doesn't have a survey attached either, so just a quick sweep of the cinema or the self checkout tills will net me a voucher almost every time. Food always tastes better when there's a discount on it!

Achievable goal: Save £24 a year

If you're a weekly shopper like me, you should get several till spit coupons with every shop. But even using a couple a month with a total value of £2, would save you £24 throughout the year. You have the potential to save a lot more however with £5 off coupons, and using discarded receipts.

Combined yearly savings: £788

Cashback apps

The era of couponing has gone digital. There are now apps on your phone which will pay you money back for doing your weekly shop. It only takes a little bit of work by taking a photo of the receipt on your smartphone, and you get your money back… pretty cool right?

All of the cashback apps work in the same way, crediting you cash back when you have shown a receipt of purchase. On each, they have a variety of products each with its own cashback amount if you buy it. You could get a fixed price cashback offer (50p for example) or even get a freebie, where you are refunded the full amount no matter the spend.

Now here's the interesting part… If you can ever find a cashback offer, to stack with a cashback offer from a different app, you can claim for both. Stacking cashback with coupons works too – so there are opportunities for some serious savings here!

Several times I have walked out of the store making profits thanks to my cashback. On one occasion I had a coupon for £1 off Kettle Chips. By stacking the coupon with a sale at Tesco (where they were priced at £1), I was already getting them for free. But imagine my excitement when I saw the exact same product also having cashback on it from one of these apps! I could claim an extra 50p back through the app CheckoutSmart too, which meant I paid £0 at the till, and claimed a bonus 50p when I snapped the receipt. Not everyday you get paid to eat crisps… but when you do, it's a very good day!

Another great example I saw recently was a deal stack on Soft and Gentle deodorant. It was on sale at Asda for £1, and you could print off a 50p off coupon and use a 50p cashback offer on the CheckoutSmart app, which made it completely free. One of the cool things about this, was you could claim the cashback on CheckoutSmart up to 10 times – so if you had several computers to print out more than one coupon, you could get several freebies.

This just shows you how using your coupon savings can add up by using these apps. I'm sure you'd love to know what they are and how they work, so here they are:

CheckoutSmart

This is the most popular cashback app that regularly offers freebies, giving you the full cost of the product back as cashback (and if you can stack those to coupons - you're golden!).

As of writing this, there are currently 37 cashback offers, with two of them being for free items - Mountain Dew and Moma Porridge. With quite a lot of these offers, you can redeem them at any supermarket you like, but it may vary per deal.

If you are an online shopper, this app also allows you to claim cashback on your online shopping too, by scanning a picture of your receipt when your shopping is delivered (something the other apps don't do). Be sure to check with each offer that you can use them at the online supermarkets however (look for the full website URLs such as 'Tesco.com').

Your cashback will collect into your CheckoutSmart account and you can redeem your money by bank transfer at any time – however you'll be charged a 5% processing fee if you do before you have earned £20. With rolling freebies on this app, it shouldn't take you very long to earn more than £20 and not have to pay the fees.

> *Tip: Most CheckoutSmart offers allow you to claim cashback more than once too. This means if you see a really good deal with cashback, you can stock up on more than one.*

Shopmium

Shopmium works in a very similar way to CheckoutSmart. There are lots of offers for you to choose from, with the only difference being, once your cashback claims are approved, you don't need to withdraw any balances, they will automatically transfer the money into your PayPal or bank account. Handy for those that forget to cash out – as they do it all for you.

As of writing this, there are 7 offers on the app for you to choose from. Unfortunately you can only claim each one once, however the offers are generally updated each week, which means there should be something new to claim quite frequently. Be sure to check with each offer which supermarket it is redeemable at, as some of them are store specific (even down to which city you shop in).

> *Tip: On Shopmium, there is a geo-locater on each offer that allows you to see the closest supermarket the offer can be used at.*

Green Jinn

This is the newest cashback app and offers are currently only available at Tesco, Sainsbury's and Waitrose. It has a nifty personalisation option, where you select what items you'd be interested in cashback on, and they personalise your selection of offers in the app (which is handy if you don't want to see pet food offers if you don't have a pet).

Like the other two apps, just a picture of the receipt will yield you the cashback into your account, which you will need to manually claim. You can claim at any time with no fee and transfer the money through PayPal or bank transfer.

Tip: With cashback apps, it's always worth checking them around key times of year such as Pancake Day, Easter and Halloween, as there are often exclusive offers for pancakes, chocolate eggs and pumpkins. Quite often on CheckoutSmart, you can pick up something for free.

Achievable goal: Save £26 a year

Check the apps before you go shopping to see if anything matches what you have on your list. If you can get 50p cashback from one offer per weekly shop, you'd save £26 a year. If you take advantage of the freebie offers through the apps, it could add up to a lot more.

Combined yearly savings: £814

Online coupon codes

Most of the coupon tips so far only apply to in store shopping, but there are still ways to save money if you're an online grocery shopper too, and it's down to online codes. There are always codes floating around to save you money on your shopping, whether you are a new customer or not - and some can save you up to £20 on your shop.

New customer codes

At any given time, there are loads of new customer codes floating around to get you money off your online shop. Quite often they are blanket money off codes such as £15 off your first £60 spend, so it is quite a substantial discount. With the amount of online grocery retailers, it is unlikely you've shopped with them all (if any), which means if you didn't fancy going out for your shopping one week, you can take it in turns to rinse new customer codes of the supermarkets you haven't used.

All of the big supermarkets including Sainsbury's, Tesco, Asda, Morrisons, Ocado, Waitrose and Iceland all have online grocery services with discount codes that circulate. If you haven't got an account with any of these supermarkets, you can save a large amount by cycling through them all one by one.

Of the supermarkets mentioned above, Sainsbury's, Waitrose and Ocado host their own new customer codes on their site frequently (if not all of the time), and you can often get extra perks such as a free delivery pass if you use their codes too.

To find new customer codes for the other supermarkets, all it takes is a quick Google search most of the time. Online voucher websites such as MyVoucherCodes.co.uk and VoucherCodes.co.uk usually feature codes from the supermarkets if there is one available. There may not be one around all of the time, but you should find one eventually.

Here is a break down of what kind of discounts you can get with each supermarket. These offers can vary, so may be slightly different by the time you're reading this, but these are the ones I usually see. If you use them all, you could net yourself up to £175 in savings – and you don't even have to leave the front door!

Waitrose up to £100 off (across 5 shops)

If you know you'll be doing big online shops over the next few weeks (or don't feel like going in store for your shopping), Waitrose has a generous new customer offer that usually sits on their website. They'll give you £20 off your shop each week when you spend between £80-£100 for five weeks after your initial sign up. Usually it's £20 off your first shop of £80 or more, then for the next four weeks, it's £20 off a £100 spend, though this can vary.

That may sound like a lot to spend, however getting 20-25% off your shopping is not to be sniffed at, especially since it's just a simple code. Spending £100 a week on shopping might be a bit too much for some families, in which case it might be worth just doing the initial sign up bonus at a lower spend. But for big families who have a lot of mouths to feed, it could save you £100 off your shopping over 5 weeks, and you don't even have to leave the house.

If you have the money to do so, and you still want to take advantage of the weekly £20 off codes, it might be worth looking at their prices of non perishable items such as toilet paper, shampoo and body wash. If there is a decent offer on those products, which you can stack with the code, it might be worth stocking up on the essentials - especially if there is no expiry date on them. Yet another way to continue to save, and why potentially pay full price for them later, when you can stock up now at a cheap price today?

Sainsbury's £15 off £60 spend

Sainsbury's host their codes on their website, though you may be able to find stronger offers on other voucher sites such as MyVoucherCodes, so it's always worth checking.

Usually you would find a £15-20 off code for a £60-80 spend, depending on what time you look. One of the most common (and strongest offers) is £15 off a £60 spend, which is a 25% saving.

A lot of savvy shoppers usually stack this new customer code with a 25% off wine deal, that Sainsbury's hold every couple of months or so. In this deal, when you purchase 6 bottles on wine, prosecco or champagne, you get 25% off of them, and with the code on top too, it makes for some cheap bubbly. Some offers have yielded bottles of prosecco for as little as £1.66 each bottle, which is a corking deal (sorry!).

Ocado £20 off £80 spend + one years free delivery

Ocado's discount code usually comes with the added bonus of a free years 'smart pass', which gets you free delivery for a year, exclusive offers, priority Christmas delivery and free samples (which is a nice perk to have). The code itself should get you 25% off your first shop (usually with a minimum spend of £80, and max reward of £20... so practically it's a £20 off £80 spend code - but they don't advertise it as that). Be sure to have a look on Google for any over offers with lower minimum spends and higher discounts, because they do crop up.

All in all, it's a pretty good deal, considering the cost of delivery can really add up for online shoppers too. If you had a week where you just wanted to order online, and didn't have a coupon, but had the free delivery through Ocado, you could still save that way. Minimum spend requirements on Ocado are quite low at only £40, so it could be a good option if you wanted to be a casual couponer!

Asda £10 off £50 spend

The new customer codes at Asda when they roll around are actually quite good value. Its minimum spend is usually lower than the rest of the supermarkets, with still a decent discount. The most common code you'd find is £10 off a £50 spend on your first order, which equates to 20% savings. These pop up on voucher code websites, and are often hotly discussed on deals forums such as HotUKDeals and MoneySavingExpert.

If you have downloaded the Asda App for your smartphone or tablet, there have been new customer offers pop up on there too recently. The most prominent being £6 off a £40 spend, which although is a smaller discount at 15%, is great for those who don't need to spend a lot on shopping, or only need a little top up shop.

Tesco £15 off £60 spend

Tesco grocery codes do crop up, but they aren't as readily available as most of the others. You'd usually find these as exclusive offers on one of the main voucher sites, and would usually be a £15 off a £60 spend code, which nets you a 25% discount. It's worth looking around popular times of year for online shopping, such as the start of January (when belts are tight) and big yearly events such as Easter, Halloween and Christmas, as these are the times when Tesco releases codes more frequently to attract more customers.

It's worth mentioning too that on Tesco's website, they offer a free months trial of its 'Delivery Saver' scheme, which gets you free delivery and priority delivery slots for a month, which can be quite handy.

> *Tip: If you do sign up, they automatically enroll you onto the paid monthly membership when the trial expires, so be sure to cancel if you don't want to pay monthly.*

Iceland £10 off £60 spend

Until recently, I didn't even know that Iceland had online shopping, so a lot of people might have never used an online discount code from Iceland. They don't pop up all of the time, but when they do, you will find them on external voucher websites. The saving will amount to around 18% off, which is decent if you didn't have any coupons to use for that week.

Spending more than £35 online at Iceland gives you free next day delivery too, which is quite a good perk. The added saving from free delivery makes this one to look at if you haven't shopped there.

Morrison's £5 off £80 spend

And finally the worst for last... I've done this wrong haven't I! Morrison's online codes don't pop up all that often, and when they do, the one I see the most is only £5 off an £80 spend (a measly 6% saving). Sometimes you might see a higher discount code on the voucher sites, but it hasn't been a while since I've seen a very strong Morrison's offer. Of course, a saving is a saving, but there are better deals to be had.

So those are the new customer codes you might see. Obviously, there is one obvious catch with these codes... you have to be a new customer to use them. But even if you have an online shopping account with any of those supermarkets, there may still be a way you can use the codes in your household to save some money...

If you have more than one person in your household, depending on the T&Cs of each code, you may be able to sign up your spouse, relative or housemate to use the offer as well. Some codes state that it is 'one code to be used per person', so if you live with more than one person in your household, you can use the code again on a new account with the other person's name. Using this across every single grocery website with online codes will keep your kitchens stocked for quite a while, that's for sure! The phrase to watch out for is 'per household'. If you see that in the T&Cs of a code, and you already have an account, then unfortunately you can't use it – but it's always worth checking.

Now I'm not suggesting you use all of these codes at once (who can eat that many groceries?) but if you are a new customer to all of these sites, you can net yourself £175 when they are all completed. You can easily space out each online delivery throughout the year, as there are 7 different supermarkets with codes to choose from. Besides the Waitrose offer, where you have to shop there each week to get the next code, you can space them out to monthly or bi-monthly to get the most out of them over the year. If you have never shopped online, there is £175 worth of value in all of these codes, which is a massive amount of cash.

Achievable goal: Save £50 in total

I've made this goal as realistic as possible, as not everyone will be able to get the full £175 due to already being a member. You can easily extract £50 from these, either with only the first Waitrose, Asda and Iceland codes… or the Ocado, Tesco and Sainsbury's codes. However you want to (or can) do it. If you can sign up for more and get a higher value off, by all means, but it may not be possible for most who already have accounts. These can easily be spread out over the year, but once you have used them, it won't be repeatable year after year.

Combined yearly savings: £864

Discount codes for everyone

Whether you're a new customer or not, there are also several ways to use codes to save you money on your online shop - and some of them involve freebies - which everybody loves! Most of these codes come from Tesco and Sainsbury's, so regular online shoppers can take advantage week after week.

Sainsbury's online codes

Quite often, Sainsbury's will release codes to get things for free when shopping online. You'll find them under the 'discover' tab on the Sainsbury's grocery website on a page called 'freebies and competitions'.

If you see an item on there that you want, click on it to receive the code, and be able to add it to your basket. Once you've finished shopping, enter the code in the discount codes section, before you purchase.

If there is more than one freebie on the page that you'd like to use, just enter all of the codes for freebies you want to use before you checkout (but be sure you have them in your basket or the codes won't work).

Most of these codes have a maximum number of redemptions and a set expiry date, so be sure to use them quick if you see something you want.

As of writing, there is a code for a free fajita mix for the first 10,000 people. Just by checking there before you completed your online shopping can give you another option for dinner – that didn't cost you a penny. In the past, I have seen codes for free flowers, baby food and bread, but it's worth noting that the popular items with a limited number available tend to go fast.

Achievable goal: Save £24 a year

Use one of these freebie offers a month with your shopping online, and save £24 a year. Quite often these freebie offers are released together at once, so if you wanted to, you could fill up your basket with freebies, and save a lot more.

Combined yearly savings: £888

Tesco online codes

Tesco also offers codes for money off their products too, but they usually aren't as high value. Do you remember the free in store Tesco magazine that comes out every month? The coupons featured inside also have online codes written on each one for online shoppers.

These will be money off coupons for specific products, but a new magazine comes out monthly, so if there is nothing that takes your fancy one month, there will be different ones the next.

The coupons will be found in the front page of the Tesco magazine, and the online codes for each coupon are written into the T&Cs. Each coupon is only one use per transaction, but if you shop weekly and there is a coupon in there for something you buy regularly, then you can use the code each time you shop until it expires.

Similarly, if you get sent any Clubcard coupons in the post, they will all have online codes on them too. Whether it's £1 off a product, a £5 off 'helping hand' coupon or your actual Clubcard earnings, they can all be used online (though I wouldn't use your Clubcard earnings on regular shopping, as you don't get the best value there).

Achievable goal: Save £12 a year

Use one of these coupons with your online shopping order a month and save £12 a year.

Combined yearly savings: £900

Competitions

A fun, yet not guaranteed way to get your hands on some coupons, is through competitions. Brands will often hold prize draws or comment competitions on their social media accounts and through newsletters, giving away coupons and free prizes. By signing up to your favourite brands and entering your name and email address, you have the chance of winning freebies. On social media, sometimes just a like and comment could bag you a freebie coupon. I've earned hundreds of pounds worth of coupons by doing this over the years. You've got to be in it to win it - right?

Just in the past month of writing this, I've earned a free pizza coupon from Ristorante, a free pack of Taste Inc chicken and three free packs of Kabuto noodles just from commenting on their Facebook page competitions. Approximately £10 in value that I earned in just a week - with a little bit of luck!

Some brands are better than others at holding competitions, and there are several you can find offering freebie coupons as prizes on a regular basis on social media. It's worth following brands that you like, so you don't miss out on any, as they may pop up at any time. Here are some of the main brands that hold them regularly:

- Ristorante Pizza
- Wyke Farm Cheese (Free Cheese Friday)
- Kabuto Noodles
- Taste Inc Chicken
- Goodfellas Pizza

- Sunny D

Achievable goal: Save £30 a year

Even if you have average luck, if you get a £5 freebie win every other month (or a small £2.50 win every month), you'd have £30 a year extra in your pocket.

Combined yearly savings: £930

Other places to find coupons

Aside from the main ways mentioned above, coupons can crop up randomly in other places, where it is worth keeping an eye out for them.

Wombling

Disclaimer: As this is an 'ultimate' guide to couponing, I have included this tip, yet the legalities of this are yet to be confirmed. Use your own judgement as to whether you partake in this method.

Have you ever heard of the term 'Wombling'? It is the practice of picking up discarded coupons and receipts, and using them for yourself. I am a Wombler... and no, I'm not from Wimbledon.

Quite often, poor unloved coupons can be found dumped with no owner around the floors, car parks and shopping trolleys of supermarkets. How anyone can do such a thing is beyond me.

Luckily for you, some of these coupons you can pick up and use for yourself the next time you shop. This only works when the coupons are not tied to loyalty cards such as Clubcard or Nectar when printed at the till.

The best supermarket to womble at is Asda, and it's all to do with their 'price guarantee' promotion, found at the bottom of Asda receipts.

If you have bought 10 or more comparable items at Asda, you can compare the price of the goods in your trolley with other supermarkets through its online tool, and if Asda is not *at least* 10% cheaper, then you get a coupon for the difference.

Being 10% cheaper in today's fierce supermarket pricing war is quite a challenge, so a lot of the time you will actually get a coupon back. You can get a maximum of £10 for each receipt – which is not to be sniffed at.

As you have to enter the details of the receipt online to do the price guarantee, most people don't check and can be missing out on free cash. So for those people that leave their receipts in their trolleys, or 'accidentally drop them' on the way to their car, you can take advantage and try their receipts too. If receipts are left in car parks, shopping trolleys or even bins – they definitely haven't been checked for coupons.

With up to £10 worth of coupons on every receipt, it's absolutely worth checking them. They aren't tied to any loyalty cards (as Asda doesn't have one), so you are able to use any earnings for yourself. If there are coupons attached, you print them out there and then and make a saving during your next shop at Asda. If there isn't, you've not lost anything. It's like coupon bingo, there's a bit of luck involved but when you score a win - it's such a rush!

I've spent many a day sleuthing around the Asda car park looking for little papers of joy, and I have had a quick look in a bin or too (but you don't have to be that extreme). I've racked up £100s worth of savings just by doing this method. One of my favourite pick ups was offering to take someone's shopping trolley back to the drop off point one time. Not only was I doing a good deed for someone – I saw two receipts at the bottom, which I hoped to grab! I managed to get my hands on them, and once checked at home, I'd scored! One had a £6 coupon attached, and the other had an £8 coupon! That's £14 I got off my next Asda shopping trip, which has no minimum spend by the way, so you can just waltz in and grab items for free. I walked out with a bag of chocolate, sweeties and cakes for free (I was a 17 year old with a very sweet tooth). If that's not karma, I don't know what is!

If you want to try your hand at wombling, here are a few tips for you:

- I'd recommend getting yourself an anti-bacterial gel, disinfectant wipes – or even gloves for your wombling adventures. You might not need them, but if any receipts have any mud or other nasties on them, would be good to have them handy. I found one caked in mud once, but still took a photo of the receipt details, and got a £1.50 coupon when I entered it in.

- The receipts to look out for (the wombling jackpot if you will) are the longer and more expensive receipts. The more items on the receipt and more spent means there is a better chance on having a high value coupon attached to it. The more products on a receipt, the more the variance in price can be between supermarkets – which is what you want for a high value price guarantee.

- Although there is no law against you wombling inside a supermarket, it is probably best to stick outside in the car park or area outside. These areas are public space, so you have free reign to go wombling. Inside a supermarket, as it is commercial grounds, someone has control of what happens in there. Again, there is no law against wombling inside a shop, but if someone doesn't like what you are doing, you could be told to stop or escorted out. On public space, you're free to womble as you please!

Events

At big events such as roadshows, you might find coupons being handed out in goody bags or along with free samples as you are wandering around. Usually if you see someone handing out a freebie, it's usually accompanied with a money off coupon for your next purchase.

It's always worth checking to see if there are any lurking around events such as the Ideal Home Show, Good Food Show and Vegan Food Fest to name a few - there are often multiple coupons for you to collect.

And with most of these shows, free tickets and freebie coupon codes are widely available - so you can coupon your way to getting more coupons! Coupon-ception!

If you can't get to any big events such as these, it's not uncommon to find freebie or coupon distributors in public places too. Whenever you are in your local town centre of shopping mall, outside popular underground stations in London or at major train stations around the country, you may see someone giving away something for free. They pop up from time to time, usually to get you to try a new flavour or product or new release.

Most of the time, samples will only be small, but it's not unheard of to get full size freebie products. I once had this at my local town centre, where there were people handing out free full size bottles of Mountain Dew… but there wasn't just one person handing them out, there were several people handing them out every 20 metres you walked. As a cheeky 18 year old, I would take one, put it in my bag and move on to the next one. After a while, my bag was weighing me down – I had around 15 freebie bottles in there, with a total value of around £20! There is no hard and fast rule of how many you could take, and there were enough for everyone, so I managed to snag myself a months supply… and a very sore arm from carrying them all!

Achievable goal: Save £10 a year

Go to one event a year and pick up £5 worth of freebies and £5 worth of samples. Alternatively, grab a coupon off flyer distributers in the town centre once a month.

Combined yearly savings: £940

Bus tickets/cash machines

Not a certainty with this one, but it's always worth a look. The bus company 'First' may offer promotions and coupons on the back of your bus tickets (depending on what part of the country you live in). The most common one you might find are the £1.99 McDonalds meal coupons. Worth sticking in your pocket just in case, if you do get one.

Similarly, if using a cash machine at a supermarket, sometimes printed on the back of your balance receipt, you may see a coupon. This has happened a few times at my local Tesco when withdrawing money. There was once a coupon on the back for £1 off Birds Eye Inspirations (which when I checked in store was half price at £1.25 - SCORE!).

So those are the ways of getting your hands on coupons. As you have seen, there is never just one answer to the question "where do you find coupons?". They are everywhere!

It's all well and good knowing where the coupons are, but to really save some serious cash, you'll need to know how to use them effectively to maximise your savings. Knowing how to use them properly could mean the difference between a free shopping trip and paying a lot more...

How to use coupons effectively

After reading about where to find them, you might want to grab a stack of coupons and go wild in the aisles… but don't reach for your coat just yet. The real couponing savings don't actually come from the coupons themselves… it's the power of using them in the right place at the right time.

Using coupons alone can save you money, but if you want to push it even further, there are several techniques you can use to save even more, potentially get things for free or even make a 'profit'. By knowing how to use them effectively, you could double your savings, and trust me, there is no better feeling than walking out of the supermarket with free treats. Everything tastes better when it's free!

How do you get products for free?

It's all well and good spending a coupon on a full priced item. Yes, you'll save a bit of money, but that's not the most efficient and cost effective way to use your coupons. If you can restrain yourself from spending them right away, and waiting to use the coupon at the right time, then you could double the amount you're saving.

It's all to do with using your coupons when a product is on sale. Let me explain. An average coupon is valid for around a month, so that gives you four weeks to use it. In the major UK supermarkets, there are new sales and deals that rotate every week, sometimes twice a week. That gives you numerous chances over four weeks for the product you have a coupon for, to drop in price in at least one major supermarket.

On average, each individual item goes on sale in *at least* one of the major supermarkets every two weeks. If you find a coupon, and there are no sales or discounts on the product when you first receive it, by hanging back and waiting for a sale (and you should get one), it'll mean a massive increase to your savings. This is how you start to get products for free.

Matching a coupon to a sale, instead of using it when it's marked at full price, is how you take your couponing to the next level. Let's look at a few examples of this in practice:

If you have a £1 off coupon for a pack of butter, which is priced at £2 normally, using the £1 off coupon means you'll get it for £1. Already that is a decent saving of 50%, however you could do better. If you know that this brand goes on special offer frequently, wait for it to go half price at £1, and THEN use your £1 off coupon, then you pay nothing. It would be totally free. By waiting for a sale, instead of getting 50% off (which you can get from a half price sale), you walk out with a freebie.

Now imagine doing this several times over, the savings will really start to rocket. If a coupon value is high enough, and you know the product is something that goes on sale regularly, just that bit of patience will start to heavily reduce your weekly shopping bill.

Finding a high value coupon with a big enough discount won't happen all the time, so not *every* product you get will be free. However if you can match coupons to any kind of sale, you will still be practically doubling your discount. This is the way that the savings add up.

Coupons work on 'buy one get one free' promotions too. If you have two of the same coupon, and it's BOGOF, you can use them both (as you are buying two products). I once did this with tissue boxes. They were £2.10 each and on offer at BOGOF. By using two 50p off coupons (one on each item), I got two boxes of tissues for £1.10, when they would usually cost £4.20 for two boxes. The power of using coupons at the right time meant a huge saving.

The holy grail here is matching with more than one different coupon offer. Most coupons are only one per item (so you can't print off five coupons for a jar of coffee and make £5 from it), but if you had several types of coupons from the ways listed above, you can stack them.

For example, if you had a printed coupon that matched a cashback offer on the same product, you can use both. If you had a printed coupon and a manufacturers coupon (that happens to be on the same brand), you can use both. If you had either of those and ALSO had a £5 off £40 spend coupon, then all of them would stack.

By stacking coupons and offers like this, you have the chance to get things for free, or even have a higher value in coupons than the products you are buying... which means you could profit...

How to make a 'profit'

As I've said before, supermarkets unfortunately won't give you physical money back if your coupon total is higher than you basket value, but there is still a way to profit. It's called an 'overage'.

If you have a coupon that is worth more than the value of the product you're buying, then the difference is called an 'overage' and can be used as credit against the rest of your shopping. For example, if you have a coupon for £1 off chocolate, and its price is 50p, the extra 50p can be used against the rest of your shopping.

Why does this happen? Each coupon scans in at face value, thanks to the programmed barcode. This means, if you have a £1 off coupon, as long as you buy the product that it's advertising, it will scan through at £1 regardless of the price it is in that supermarket. Because of this, you can use the extra money as credit off the rest of your shopping.

The way to maximise this, is to use your overage to buy products where discounts are limited. Items such as fruit and veg, meat or even alcohol can be bought alongside overage to get money off them too. If you are doing a big shop, and you know for a fact your total isn't going to hit £0, you can just use the overage off the rest of your shopping, without adding anything.

The best type of coupon for getting you an item for free with an overage, are those from manufacturers. These are often high value coupons, more than covering the cost of a single product, so if you can find it on sale too, then you can claim a freebie and an overage.

I once took advantage of overage in a very weird way, but only weird because of the product I was buying...! There was a coupon for £1 off Nair hair removal cream on their website. You could use it on any product, including the cheapest sachets at just 80p. So for each one I bought with a coupon, I made 20p overage. Thus begun a mass of badgering all of my friends to print off these hair removal coupons for me (they must have thought I had a serious hair problem!). I managed to print out 10 coupons, and bought 10 sachets of hair removal cream... (who knows what was going through the cashier's head!). In total, my overage was £2 - which I used to get some free strawberries. I still have that receipt proudly sitting in my room with a mass of hair

83

remover, one pack of strawberry's and a £0 total on it. If anyone wants some hair removal sachets… they are still in my stockpile. You can have them for free!

If you get any elusive freebie coupons, you can often profit with overage on these too. If the coupon is programmed to scan at the item's full price, and you happen to find that product on sale, then you will get the extra money back off of your shopping. A freebie and a profit – what could be better?

Supermarket comparison sites

There is a website for couponers and savvy shoppers alike called MySupermarket.co.uk. MySupermarket shows you all of the current prices on everything you could possibly buy in all of the major supermarkets. It's the 'Go Compare' for groceries if you will.

Using something like this saves a lot of time by not having to go to each individual supermarket's website to check the prices. You can also create your shopping trip online with the items you're going to buy, and it will tell you how much it would cost in each supermarket. It's a handy tool for my coupon trips. I type in every product I have a coupon for (as long as it's not specific to one supermarket) and whichever comes out cheapest, that's where I head to! This way I know down to the penny how much it should cost, and then how much after coupons with a little bit of maths!

With your online basket, you can click through directly to that supermarket's website with the items you just compared, so all you'd have to do is select delivery and pay. This is quite a handy feature if you maybe don't feel like couponing that week (if there ever is such a feeling!).

You can also claim cashback as part of your shop. They have a cashback section of their website, which allows you to earn money back on your shopping if you buy the groceries through them. Once purchased, you will be able to withdraw the cashback from their site through PayPal.

Predicting sales

If you want to be an undercover couponing aficionado, it's actually possible for you to predict the next supermarket sale to use your coupon with. Several features on MySupermarket allow you to monitor pricing and see if items are at their lowest price.

Once you've selected a product you want to check prices for, and you've selected your supermarket of choice, it will tell you whether it is above or below the average price. If it is below, then it's usually a good time to pounce and use your coupon. If it's not, then it might be worth holding off, as sales generally come round every two weeks or so on most products.

If it's not on sale and you want to be alerted for when a new one comes along, if you are signed in, you can opt in for email price alerts for when the price changes. This means if you have a coupon for something, and you are signed up to alerts, you will definitely get the cheapest price when the sale comes round. Just make sure that your coupon doesn't expire while you are waiting for a sale. If one doesn't come, and you still need that product, then you can still make a saving just by using the coupon on its own (wasting them is very painful!).

Coupon terms & conditions

Now you know how to find coupons, it's important to know how they work once you get to the supermarket, to avoid any pushback from cashiers. Each supermarket has a different store policy when it comes to coupons and each coupon has different terms and conditions. Most of them are straight forward, but it's good to know beforehand what they all mean.

Common terms and conditions

Each coupon has T&Cs on them, and while most have the same spiel, it can be confusing as to its meaning. Here are the most common things you'll see on a coupon and it's meaning in easier to understand English!

"One coupon per product purchased" - You can only use one coupon per individual product, AKA you can't use two of the same coupon on one individual item. If you have 10 coupons all for the same cereal brand, you'll have to buy 10 cereal boxes to use them all.

"One coupon per transaction" - You can only use one of those particular coupons in a receipted transaction. There is a way around this however, by splitting your shopping trip into different transactions by using the dividers you find at checkout.

"One coupon per customer" - Pretty self explanatory, but if you go shopping with your spouse or children, they count as another person… so you can use as many as there are people with you.

"Cannot be used in conjunction with any other offer" - This is a confusing one, with many debating over its meaning. Depending on who you ask (including supermarkets themselves), you'd get a different answer. Some saying it means it can't be used with other coupon offer, and others saying it means it can't be used with in store promotions.

I can't give you a straightforward answer as to which one is correct, so let me give you the facts. Coupons that have this in their T&Cs still work, even if scanned through on a discounted item in all supermarkets. With offers rotating in the supermarkets so frequently, sometimes you have no other option than to use a coupon when there is a deal on - or they both expire.

Because of this, I believe that it refers to usage with other coupon offers, but this is hard to definitively prove. If you use a coupon on a promotion when it says this in its T&Cs, the only time you might run into a problem is if cashiers stop and read the small print, and its hard to explain.

Supermarket coupon policies

Depending on where you shop, there may be different policies relating to how coupons can be used at their store. For the most part, the big supermarkets will accept all coupons, so long as you buy the product that the coupon features. There are a few exceptions to this however, with a few of the smaller supermarkets having stricter guidelines.

Tesco couponing policy

Accepts all coupons including printable, manufacturers and store coupons, the only exception being, you can't use Sainsbury's coupons at Tesco (for obvious reasons). You can use as many coupons as you'd like per transaction with the exception of the 'helping hand' coupons of £5 off £40 spends, where the limit is one per transaction (but easily avoidable by splitting transactions up if necessary). All coupons can be used on discounted products such as sale items and items further reduced by yellow stickers, so long as the coupons are for the product that is reduced.

Asda couponing policy

The Asda couponing policy works the same way as Tesco. You can use any coupons you like, with no limit to how many you can use per transaction. You can use coupons on discounted products as well as yellow sticker products too, as long as the coupon matches the item you are purchasing. As long as you adhere to the coupon T&Cs, there shouldn't be any problems.

Sainsbury's couponing policy

The same again. So long as you stick to the T&Cs as set out by each coupon, you can use as many as you'd like in each transaction, and all coupons are accepted. You can use coupons on discounted products too including yellow stickers.

Waitrose couponing policy

Sensing a theme here? You can again use as many as you like, so long as the T&Cs are met. The only exception to this rule are £5 off £40 spend coupons where the limit is one per transaction. Using coupons on discounted products such as yellow stickers and in store discounts is fine, as long as the coupon matches.

Morrison's couponing policy

Slightly different this time, but the same principles still apply. You can use as many coupons as you like in one transaction, as long as T&Cs are adhered too. The only change here being, you can't use coupons on already discounted products such as yellow stickers. You are still able to use coupons on sale items, but if a product is on knockdown, you can't stack them.

Aldi couponing policy

Here's where things start to change. Aldi does not accept printable, manufacturers and other forms of coupon. The reason for this is mostly because their products are off-brand items anyway. The only kind of coupon it will accept is Aldi issued coupons for only their stores, which are mostly the £5 off £40 spend coupons you will find in newspapers. You are able to split your transactions up if you have more than one coupon however. Aldi coupons are hard to come by anyway, and these £5 off offers don't pop up too much.

Lidl couponing policy

Due to selling off-brand items similar to Aldi, Lidl also doesn't accept coupons, apart from the £5 off £40 spends in the newspapers. You are able to split your transactions up if you have more than one coupon, but that is as far as it gets.

Those are the main supermarket policies, and I hope they are fairly easy to understand. Mostly, if you just follow the coupon T&Cs, you'll be fine. If you shop at any other supermarket, it might be worth sending a quick email to ask about their in store couponing policy before you go shopping. The last thing you want is to be turned away at checkout from using them.

Profit when things go wrong

In the unlikely event that you have trouble claiming coupons in your chosen supermarket, you can actually play this to your advantage to earn even more coupons from it. On some occasions when using coupons, even if you know the T&Cs inside and out, the cashiers that serve you might not be as clued up as you'd like. There may be occasions when you're told you can't use certain coupons, just for the fact that the cashier doesn't understand how they work.

If this happens on any occasion at any supermarket, where you know you've used them legitimately and been turned away - you can be compensated for it. Remember all about how complaining pays? Send an email to head office explaining the situation, and that you were in the right, and you will likely be sent a gift card for the inconvenience. This works at all the major supermarkets, and by reporting which store didn't know about how coupons work, head office can prompt managers to train staff, so it shouldn't happen again.

If a coupon for a certain product is rejected by the cashier, you can politely ask for them to remove that item from your bill - and use the coupon next time to get the money off. Just another way to earn coupons, from coupons… from coupons. It's coupon-ception!

Stockpiling

Yes – I have a stockpile (can you blame me?). A stockpile is basically a collection of items that you get for free or cheap with coupons that you save for a rainy day. At one point, my stockpile was so big, I couldn't open my spare bedroom door because there was so much cheap stuff in there that I'd stored! I'm talking six months worth of toothbrushes, around 20 packs of Velvet tissues (which I dubbed 'the leaning tower of tissues') and 24 packs of loo roll that cost me £4.80 for them all. It may sound a bit mad, but I can explain why…

Everything in my stockpile room I got at a bargain price, and if it was something that we as a family used, it was worth getting more than one. My rule of thumb for stockpiling is – if it's more than 60% off the RRP, then I'd stockpile and get more than one. The reason for this, is you can often find items at half price, so if you can stack with a coupon to boost your savings past 60%, there won't be many occasions to get this level of discount.

My life motto for stockpiling is 'why pay full price later, when it is free or cheap today?'. If you can pick up toothpaste that normally costs £2 for just 50p per tube, why would you not get more than one? Especially on products like this, that will always be used in the household, and you get through a lot of on a yearly basis.

There are some exceptions to stockpiling however…

I recommend only stockpiling the things that don't have an expiry date. Trying to stockpile food or drink might mean it goes out of date, and that is just money wasted. If you stick to things that don't expire and are non-perishable such as toilet paper, shampoo, toothbrushes, toothpaste, cleaning products and tissues – then you will never have that issue. Plus it's quite nice to have your own personal supermarket of goodies stored away when you need it.

> *Tip: There are certain foods that can be stockpiled in the fridge or freezer such as cheese, bread and butter (if you have room).*

It's important to only stockpile things that you'll actually use. Don't make the mistake of buying tons of cat food if you don't have a cat. I know it sounds like common sense, but when you are in the whacky world of couponing, it's easy to get carried away!

When I first started couponing, I remember being super excited at buying 'ladies products' for just 50p per pack with coupons I had. I thought mum would be able to use them and get through them, so I bought about 10 packs to put in our stockpile room. Little did I know… they weren't feminine hygiene products like I first thought… they were incontinence pads...! Imagine the look on my mother's face when I excitedly showed her what I stockpiled, and they were for incontinence! Safe to say, her excitement didn't match mine when I thought I'd saved us a load of money, but I certainly learned my lesson – and hopefully made some people laugh from my silly mistakes!

Picking the right checkout

You have done the easy bit by going around and collecting all of your items, now comes mission coupon. Something as simple as picking the right cashier could make or break your shopping trip... I'm serious!

When I go to the checkout, I look for the happiest cashier. Sometimes I spend more time looking for the right cashier than actually shopping itself! You tend to want to pick the person that is talking to the customers and not sitting there with a face like thunder. I tend to go for young female cashiers or young male cashiers, as I am close to their age and they can relate and respond to me easily.

Because I am a regular coupon shopper, I have actually made friends with some of the staff that run the tills at my local supermarket (shout-out to you Sandra!). This greatly helps me out, as I just go in and claim my coupons with them, as we both know how it all works. If you can form a relationship with a worker (as you'll usually be memorable using coupons every time you shop), it makes life a lot easier.

It's also good coupon etiquette to let the people behind know you have coupons before you start scanning - especially on a big coupon trip. I have had many a 'tutter' behind me who was only buying a single pint of milk, while I had about 20 coupons to claim...! Don't be discouraged by the tutters though, they are just jealous they aren't saving as much as you!

The best things come in small packages... Literally!

There are all sorts of sizes of products. Value pack, regular size, travel size and so on. But which one do you go for? The average person would probably pick the value pack, as it says 'value' in the title, but it may not be what it says on the tin.

Before you buy any product, I suggest looking for the price per 100ml/g written on the labels of each product. You would be surprised at how many times the smallest or regular products are actually better value than the so called 'value packs'. And remember, if you have multiple coupons, you can only use one coupon on the big 'value packs'… yet if you bought two smaller sizes, you can use two, meaning you'll likely save more.

Most supermarkets are tactical with how they display their items too. I was once going to buy some Herbal Essences shampoo, with four £1 off coupons to spend. I went into the supermarket and all of the Herbal Essences on the shelf had a price tag of £3.79 for 400ml. Most would be inclined to buy that because it looked like the only product. What the store obviously wasn't pushing as much, was the 200ml bottles on sale at £1.12 and hidden away at the very corner of the shelf.

If an average person with these 4 coupons bought the 400ml bottles they would have paid £11.16 for the 4 bottles. Still a £4 saving because of the coupons, but not a great price at £2.79 a bottle. So let's assume you are a clever couponer and spotted the £1.12 bottle. With four coupons you would only pay 48p for the 4 bottles. Very clever!

Now some may think you are getting less because you bought the smaller bottles, and you are right, however noting the price difference between 4 bottles of 200ml (totalling 800ml) costing 48p and 2 bottles of the 400ml (also totalling 800ml) costing £5.58, you are saving a massive £5 by buying smaller and saving nearly £15 from the original value with no coupons. That's a no brainer!

Tip: Also keep an eye out for travel size products. If the coupons fail to mention a minimum size or exclude any product, then you can use it on travel size and get the product for free, or even make an overage from it if the coupon value is high enough.

Organise yourself

It goes without saying that couponing takes some organisation. With the amount of coupons you are collecting, sales to keep track of and terms and conditions to remember, it can get a bit confusing. Hence why there are several ways you can organise yourself to streamline the process.

When it comes to organising your coupons, I have my own coupon binder that is separated into sections of dairy, frozen, household etc. This may be a bit extreme, as you can just keep them in a section in your purse if you really wanted to, but this way I know where all my coupons are at any given time. One of the main things I hear people say to me is "I left all my coupons at home", if you have a special place you keep them, you shouldn't be losing them.

When I get to the supermarket, I generally write a list of all the things I'm buying with coupons, and include any additional T&Cs that I need to be aware of. That way I don't have to be fumbling about with them while I'm in the store. Before you get to the checkout, it's worth organising your coupons ready for the cashier too. Take out any that you haven't used, make sure they are all there and keep them in a nice pile ready to hand over at checkout.

It's fair to say I can be extreme when it comes to my organisation. I have several spreadsheets telling me how much I've saved, what coupons I still have and more! You don't have to be as extreme as this, however keeping a spreadsheet of what you're saving each weekly shop is a great way to see your savings that up.

Quick Tips

That is *nearly* everything you need to know about coupons and how to use them. There is another 300 pages I could write about them, but I'd be waffling for hours!

To aid you on your couponing journey, there are a few more quick tips that I can give you, to get the most out of your coupons, that didn't fit into any categories above.

Print limits

When printing out coupons online (depending on where you print them from) you maybe able to print more than one from each computer. Coupons from the coupon dedicated websites such as SuperSavvyMe, Victoria and CaringEveryday - you can only print once. Coupons hosted on brand websites however (such as those found on coupon aggregate MoneySavingExpert.com, you might be able to print more than one.

Once your coupon is printed, try hitting the back button a few times taking you back to the 'print now' button, and seeing if it will let you click print again. I've done this numerous of times even with freebie coupons! Simply hitting the back button, click print again, and your printer gets to work... printing out even more free money. Each coupon will have a unique barcode, meaning they will be two separate coupons, and totally legit. Clever eh?

It's worth mentioning too, most coupons are one or two prints per computer... so if you have several in your household, or laptops lying around, you can print the coupons on each device (and even set up your spouse on coupon dedicated websites to print more for your family). Just another way to scale up the savings.

I often print out coupons from my home computers as well as the computers at work (but be sure to check with your boss if this is okay).

Become a coupon decoder

Did you know that you can decode your barcodes to work out how much a coupon is worth? Yes, you can be an actual decoder! All you have to do is look at the last four digits of the long and thin barcode on your coupons. The first three digits will tell you the amount it's worth, followed by a random number at the end. So for example if the numbers '0507' appeared on your coupon, it'll scan at 50p. If it reads '1007' it'll scan at £1, and so on.

This is especially handy when you have coupons for free products, because if you look at the barcode, you can tell how much it's going to scan in for. If you can tell what it's worth, then you can see if you get any overage, if the item is cheaper than the coupon's value. You may find with freebie coupons, they read '000'. If you see this, it means the cashier will need to manually enter the price of the product at the till, so be sure to have the price handy to make the process smoother.

Buying coupons is a no-no!

As coupons can be everywhere, they can also be in the wrong places. You might find coupons for sale online on auction websites such as eBay, and selling sites such as Facebook Marketplace and Gumtree. Personally, I would steer clear. You can never be too sure whether they're real or not.

There is a big market for people actually forging coupons or making printed versions of the real thing and selling them on to other people. If you buy a coupon online and try to redeem it, when it's a fake, you may be committing fraud. I wouldn't take the risk when it comes to buying coupons from other people. Work through the tips above and get them yourself.

Muting self service checkouts

I don't recommend using self service checkouts when you have coupons with you, as most of the time it's easier to get a human being to scan for you rather than a machine. However if you are using a self service checkout, or just quickly buying something in the supermarket, did you know there's a way to shut up the awful "unexpected item in bagging area" nagging voice?

On most checkouts if you look on the home screen before you press start, there should be a speaker icon with the volume setting in the bottom corner. Simply click it a few times until there is a red X showing through it. Then you can check out in peace without anyone else nagging you about where to shove your groceries! Don't worry, if the machine encounters a problem, there would still be a red flashing light to alert a staff member that you need help. It's pure bliss to check out in peace – you'll never hear "unexpected item in the bagging area" again… you're welcome!

Don't go shopping hungry

This is more of a guide based on previous experience! The last thing you want to do is load up your trolley with tempting treats that you simply picked up because you were hungry, and straying away from your list. I highly recommend eating before you go, as a full stomach might put you off spending as much.

Put your savings in a piggy bank

After you've been on your coupon shopping trips and saved £10-£15, without storing away it's hard to see those savings add up. What I quite like to do whenever I save money, is put the money saved into a piggybank. Over the year this builds up and up, and after a while I open up to see (visually) a massive amount of savings. It feels more real when you can see all the money in your hand, that you haven't put in the supermarkets pocket - all from using coupons!

Of course, if this is a bit too much you could always keep a spreadsheet to see how much you're saving, and how much more should be in your bank account, but this is a nice way to see how much you're actually saving. After a while of building it up, you can take that money and either deposit it in your savings, or pay for a nice holiday, or whatever you want - because you've earned it!

Non coupon related supermarket savings

There might be occasions where you won't be able to save money with coupons, and when this happens there is still loads of tips for when you're inside the supermarket that will save you money generally. Simply by going in at the right time, changing brands, or even changing the aisle that you are shopping from, can get you some instant savings. With these tips, you should be able to save money every time you shop - with coupons or not!

Brand switching

As you will know, the big 'name brands' of products can cost you a lot of money. If you only buy branded products, you could be paying up to 25% more for your basket than if you shopped supermarket own brand products. I know most people like to stick with the same brands, however there have been a lot of studies that show, some own brand products are made in the exact same factory or have the exact same taste as some of the branded ones.

I've tested this on numerous occasions. For example McVities digestive biscuits at Sainsbury's usually cost £1 a pack, yet the Sainsbury's own brand cost 55p for the same size. I gave both products to a group of money savers, to see which one they liked the best without telling them which is which. An overwhelming majority of 19 to 1 preferred the Sainsbury's own brand biscuit, and there was a 45p difference in the price.

But wait, there's more! Everybody loves a tube of Pringles, but at a price of £2.25 per tube, they can really add up to a lot of money if you're an addict like me! People don't know that most supermarkets offer an alternative, with Tesco's 'Chipz' only costing 85p per tube. When tested among a group of people, 15 out of 20 preferred the Tesco's own brand, and at a saving of £1.35 for each tube, if you're buying them regularly – that adds up to some serious savings. Once the price drops… you can't stop.

Now imagine doing that several times over. Even by trying one switch down every single week to see if you like that product, could mean big savings throughout the year. And if you find that you like a swap, or you think it's better than the brand, then you can make a permanent switch, and save even more.

This is a process called downshifting. For whatever level of product you buy (either 'Finest', branded, own brand or value), simply go down one brand level and test it out. You don't have to do this for your whole basket either, just trying this with one product at a time and seeing if there's any switches is worth a go. Trust me - it will add up to a lot of money in the long run.

Achievable goal: Save £26 a year

Try one switch with your weekly shop, that saves you 50p per switch and over the year, it'll add up to £26 in savings. If you make a switch and you like it and stick with it, then this will add up to a lot more!

Combined yearly savings: £966

Aisle switching

This is similar to brand switching, however it's a sneaky way that supermarkets are getting you to spend more money for practically the same products. For example, if you needed cotton swabs, the first place you'd think to check would be the health and beauty aisle. Quite often though, this isn't the cheapest place to find them. Believe it or not, stopping off at the baby aisle and picking up the same cotton buds (they're made in the same country, and look exactly the same) can be found at a cheaper price. Crazy right? And this happens for quite a few different items.

Baby aisle

For all of your basic beauty essentials, such as cotton buds and cotton wool, they can all be found at cheaper prices by buying the baby items. And at a few different supermarkets, you actually get more per pack in the baby aisle that you do in the beauty aisle.

Some of these are huge savings too, one pack of cotton buds I found in Boots cost £1.50 for 200 buds in the beauty aisle. Yet walking just an aisle away to the baby section, you could get 200 cotton buds, that looked seemingly identical just in a different pack, for 55p. A near £1 saving for practically the same thing!

There are some similar swaps you can make to. For example swapping out your expensive make up remover wipes for baby wipes, can save you up to £2 each time. Also, when it comes to petroleum jelly, buying the name brand of Vaseline in a tiny 50g pot can cost you £1.50. Yet high-tailing it to the baby aisle and finding the baby petroleum jelly, it costs £1.50 for 150g - the same price for 3x the amount! If you buy it regularly, it means you'll be paying £3 less by buying the bigger pot, and from switching aisles.

World foods

If you're a lover of international cuisine in the kitchen, you can often save money when cooking those meals just by switching to the world foods aisle. It's very easy just to go down the sauces aisle to pick up your curry sauce, yet if you live in a multicultural area that imports a lot of international products, you can often find that they are cheaper than the main brands - and more authentic too!

One key example I found, was a bottle of soy sauce at Asda. The name brand 'Amoy' will set you back £1.39 for 150ml in the regular sauce aisle. Yet by just a quick switch over to world food, you could find a massive 500ml bottle of an authentic Chinese soy sauce brand for a cheaper price of £1.29. So in this case, you're saving 10p and getting over triple the size.

Another great example is herbs and spices. A tiny pot of ground ginger (Asda's own brand), will get you only 28g for 79p. But yep, you've guessed it! In the world food section, you could get an 85g pack (again over triple the size) for a cheaper price at 60p.

So whenever you want to do some authentic international cooking, or stock up on some herbs and spices, it's always worth checking to see if the world foods aisle gives a better value.

Other aisles

There are also several other aisle swaps to take a look at when you are shopping. These may not always be cheaper, but it's worth doing a quick comparison to see whether you are getting the best deal.

First off, the meat and deli counter against the pre-packaged you'd find in the refrigerated section. On occasions you might find the same meat for a cheaper price over at the deli. It won't last as long as the pre packed, however a fresher cut if you were eating straight away, can help your wallet and your tastebuds. The same can be said for cheese. Before you cram Cathedral City into your basket, have a quick look at the fresh cuts in the deli. You can often find the same big name brands, at a cheaper price just freshly cut and in a different packaging in the deli.

If you like your juice, and don't mind a longer life version, you can often find that the 'long life' juices compared to the refrigerated ones can save you a lot of money. Own brand orange juice and UHT milk, can be bought for up to half the price of the fresh stuff, and you can stick it in the fridge when you get home to still have the same cold drink. There is usually no difference in product (even the same packaging for own brand orange/apple juices, almond milks and Ocean Spray cranberry juices), the only difference is the price and how it's made – the taste should be exactly the same.

Achievable goal: Save £12 a year

Make one aisle switch a month either with your spices or your beauty products. Saving £1 each time from the switch will add up to £12 yearly. Of course, if you make the switch more often if you're a international cooking fanatic, your savings could soar.

Combined yearly savings: £978

Yellow stickers

You might have seen me talk a lot about yellow stickers throughout this book, and if you haven't heard of them, then you're missing out! Yellow stickered items are products that have been reduced by the supermarket, normally because they're expiring that day or within the next few days – and they want to flog it. But this shouldn't stop an avid money saver, as if you snap it up quickly, and have it for your dinner that day, then you can really save a lot of money.

I'm not talking little discounts either. It's quite common to find pre-packaged ready meals that usually cost £2.50 for 10p, massive trifles and deserts for mere pennies, or even the sandwiches they made for that day's lunch, that usually cost up to 3 pounds, for just 50p. It doesn't matter if they're expiring that day or within a few days, if you eat them that night, then you're just getting a discount on it.

You can usually find the reduced sections where these yellow stickered items are held spread out across the supermarket. It varies per store, but you usually find a fridge full in the meat and ready meal section, a shelf in the snack aisle and a portion of the bakery aisle containing cut price goodies.

Supermarkets tend to start reducing their products for that day from around 5PM onwards, but this can vary per store. The closer to closing time you go, that is when you find the biggest discounts as they try to sell off any last minute goods - but be warned, the good stuff might have been snapped up by other money savers.

So the next time you're in the supermarket, look out for those magical yellow stickers, because you could really cut the price of your evening meals.

Achievable goal: Save £24 a year

If you pop in just before closing time once a month and pick up your evening ready meal for £2 cheaper each time, you'll be at a £24 saving by year end. Always worth popping your head in the reduced section whenever you go shopping, for any bargains (if you'll use them!).

Combined yearly savings: £1,002

The 'Bin One' rule

When walking around the supermarket, it's very easy to stray away from the list and pick up a packet of Jaffa Cakes to put in the trolley (as my mum so often does – which drives me mad!). With so many tempting treats around every single aisle, it may mean that your total is higher than you were expecting, if you stray from your list. So to combat this, why not try the 'bin one' rule.

Every single time you go shopping, just before you get to the checkout, have a look at what's in your basket. There's probably quite a few things that you weren't intending to buy, but picked up anyway. I know it sounds painful, but have a look at the tempting treats you've added... and simply 'bin one' - get it out of there! By using this rule and discarding one item from your trolley before you get to the checkout, then you save a little bit of cash each time.

Think about it, if you discard a pack of chocolates or pack of biscuits... even just saving 50p each time, if you're shopping every week, then that's £26 you could be saving over the year. If you write a good enough list when you go shopping, then you shouldn't go hungry and shouldn't need those extra snacks, as you already have all the food you need. Use the force... and use the 'bin one' rule!

Achievable goal: Save £26 a year

Save 50p on your weekly shop by binning one thing each time, and you'll save £26 throughout the year. If you want to be brave – you could bin more of those goodies and use what's already in your cupboard to boost this further.

Combined yearly savings: £1,028

Summary

If you've made it through this couponing guide to the end, I commend you! Who knew there was so much information about tiny pieces of paper with barcodes on it? I hope you now have the knowledge and inspiration to shave £100s or even £1,000s off your supermarket shopping year after year.

Have a think back through. What small changes can you make to your life to cut your shopping bill? Even if you only take one tip away, and use it in your daily life, my work here is done (and the savings have likely paid for this book!).

If you followed all of the achievable goals, your combined yearly savings would be £1,028. What would that money mean to you? A holiday? Mortgage deposit? Or even making yourself free from debt? No matter how you spend your savings, one thing is for sure... after a few simple changes, you can start putting money back in YOUR pocket.

Remember that supermarket coupons are only the beginning. Now you should be a master of getting a cheap frozen pizza, but there are still other aspects of your life where savings can be made. Whether it's high street shopping, travel or even your monthly bills - there's likely several ways for you to save on those too… and I may be able to help you with that in my next book…!

In the future, when you're a millionaire coupon addict, living in a massive house - with rooms full of stockpiled toilet paper… be sure to think of me!

Resources

There has been a lot of information and a lot of websites mentioned throughout this book, so to save you from flicking back through all of my waffle, here are some handy links for you:

Useful websites

- SuperSavvyMe.co.uk - P&G owned coupon website
- Victoria.co.uk - P&G owned coupon website
- CaringEveryday.co.uk - Johnson & Johnson owned coupon website
- MoneySavingExpert.com/deals/coupons - A collection of all the current online coupons on the market, extracted from brand websites
- MySupermarket.co.uk - Grocery comparison website. Also allows you to set alerts for when products go on sale
- Asda.com/BrandGuarantee - The place to input your 'wombled' Asda receipts to claim coupons from
- Sainsburys.co.uk/freebies - Where Sainsbury's online shopping freebies with codes would be held.
- VoucherCodes.co.uk - Where to look for supermarket new customer codes

- MyVoucherCodes.co.uk - Another voucher website to look up new customer sign up codes

Mobile phone apps

- CheckoutSmart - Cashback app (iOS & Android)
- Shopmium - Cashback app (iOS & Android)
- GreenJinn - Cashback app (iOS & Android)
- StoCard - Mobile loyalty card storer (iOS & Android)
- MySupermarket App - Grocery comparison app, which allows you to scan items in the supermarket for pricing (iOS & Android)

Coupon Facebook pages to follow
- Jordon Cox (Follow me!)

- MSE Deals

- Latest Free Stuff

- Latest Deals

- Extreme Couponing and Cash back UK

- Savvy Deals UK

- Extreme Couponing & Bargains UK

- Extreme Couponing & Deals UK

- Coupon Clippers UK

- Total Couponery

- The Couponing Squirrel, In A Nut Shell

- Coupon Mama UK

About the author

Jordon Cox is Britain's Coupon Kid, who has been saving himself money and teaching others how to do the same since 15. With over £5,000 of supermarket savings under his belt, he has turned his attention to spreading the word on coupons, and how using them can mean a massive amount of savings for struggling families.

Jordon regularly appears on mainstream television and radio shows as a money or couponing expert, giving advice on how to find the best bargains. His biggest media escapades include getting a £600 shop for just 4p and donating it all to a charity, and finding it £8 cheaper to get from Sheffield to Essex – by flying via Berlin, Germany, rather than taking a UK train.

Jordon is a blogger for MoneySavingExpert.com (the UK's biggest financial website), freelance writer, public speaker and financial coach, whose mission is to save as many people money as possible.

To get in touch with Jordon, you can visit JordonCox.com, email jordon@JordonCox.com, Tweet @Jordon_Cox on Twitter, follow Jordon Cox on Facebook.

Printed in Poland
by Amazon Fulfillment
Poland Sp. z o.o., Wrocław

50276934R00065